THE
Ravenous
Muse

THE
Ravenous
Muse

A TABLE OF DARK
AND COMIC CONTENTS,
A BACCHANAL OF BOOKS

Karen Elizabeth Gordon

PANTHEON BOOKS • NEW YORK

Permissions acknowledgments are on pp. 233–240.

Library of Congress Cataloging-in-Publication Data

Gordon, Karen Elizabeth.
Ravenous muse / Karen Elizabeth Gordon.
p.   cm.
ISBN 0-679-41861-X
1. Food—Anecdotes.   2. Food—Quotations, maxims, etc.
I. Title.
TX357.G576   1996
641—dc20   95-24356
                                                  CIP

Book design by Fearn Cutler

Manufactured in the United States of America
First Edition
2 4 6 8 9 7 5 3 1

For Rasko

Acknowledgments

Thanks and *vielen Danke* to a sequence of translators and go-betweens who helped me capture Der Rabe: my cousins in the Tyrol, Wolfgang and Trudi Pircher, Kirstin Pauka, Annemarie Staeger, Adelaide Schafer, Ansis Darzins, Maia Gregory, Claire Wedema, Lan Nhat Nguyen, and Nadja Kossack. Nikolaus Heidelbach, the crow's creator and my bemused correspondent, I thank especially much. Haffmans Verlag graciously agreed to share him with me and kept me current with Der Rabe's metamorphoses, his ingenious uses for books.

Pat Nolan set me off on a track years ago that shows its traces here, with Queneau, Cendrars, and Roussel. Barbara Hodgson faxed me words of Joyce and Durrell. With Boris Lopatin I ate many pelmeyni with caviar and talk of Olesha, Gogol, Grin. Jean-Jacques Passera, John Hennessey, Holly Johnson, Jann Donnenwirth, Maureen Jung, Bob Baldock, and Catherine Maclay let me into their libraries and wished me *bon courage*, as did Paul Walker and my mother, Camilla Collins, ever responsive and curious.

In Paris, Danielle Mémoire introduced me to Flann O'Brien, and with Guillaume Pineau des Fôrets, Jean, and Gabriel, gave me a bed, cantatas, and desk. The bliny master of rue de Bretagne always made the trip worthwhile en route to the Bibliothèque Nationale, and when I told him, "You have the best bliny in Paris," he replied with pleasure, "I know." And speaking of pleasure, adding warmth and generosity, Marisa Mascarelli made my latest long stay in Paris possible, for which I am most grateful. Alain Bloch and Olive of Mas Lafont offered a lovely house, *très rigolo*, fountains, donkey, and music during several euphoric weeks of writing, my first in the South of France. Rastislav Mrazovac, crazy about the impulse of this book, multiplied my own devotion.

My editor, Shelley Wanger, has given me all along such fine suggestions and understanding that she is now an honored member of the Slavic Gastronomes.

THE
Ravenous
Muse

Introduction

This assembled presence of high-voltage imaginations
feels like it's always been with me, through travels in
the night, travels from one time to another, and the
geographical displacements that make my life jump far-
ther and deeper, attaching me where I belong. Many of
these writers belong together because wherever I am, so
are they: my home. Passages from books are part of my
passages across ocean and land, moving me, tying me
into a culture and place, into friendships distant and
close.

My first winter in Paris, twelve years ago, was cold
and grim not only from the winds slashing off the
Seine, but also because my dearest friend and collaborator, Carol Dunlop, had just died in that city she'd
given me, and I'd returned to Paris from London too

late, crossing the English Channel with a large black cat who drank vodka and walked on his hind legs (you'll meet him in his whiskered splendor shortly): I was reading Bulgakov's *The Master and Margarita*. So I came back to Paris in Slavic mode, and the tone was set for the years to follow and for the book you hold in your hands. Inevitably, I landed in a Balkan inn pretending to be a French hotel and moved into the Emily Dickinson Room, as I called it, for a mournful solitude. But the muse was watching over me, tossing me books and a dream that still holds sway. As punishment for a faceless offense, I was handed over to an attractive stranger who fed me Balkan dishes and taught me the Slavic tongues. I could hardly contain my delight! My life had at last begun. It was also during this winter in Paris that a letter about a Russian greyhound arrived from Beograd, written by a new friend, Silvia, whom you'll meet very soon in "El Masoquista, Brave Old Planet": Carol had brought us together.

So this book goes back that far and through sojourns since, mostly in Paris, but for one curious detour in 1988 that added the missing ingredient, the catalyst I had long awaited. Even there the Slavs were calling the shots. Headed for Eastern Europe, I was waylaid by my jaw in the Tyrol and Bavaria, where a two-step operation kept me through the autumn. At a museum restaurant in Munich, a new friendship came along: Annemarie Staeger, a Berliner with a place in

Bad Tölz too. While visiting her in Bad Tölz, I bought Annemarie a book by Bruno Schulz at Beim Winzerer, the town's finest bookstore and salon. And that brings us to the character on the cover who enticed you to touch these words. For it was he who carried the book under *my* wing, as I discovered when we returned to Annemarie's and I reached for the bag to bring out her present, took one look into the crow's eyes, and fell seriously in love.

In Paris a month later, I sent Johanna Zantl of Beim Winzerer Deutsche marks and entreaties to send me more bags emblazoned with that winsome image, the mascot of a Swiss publisher. And from Amerika, the following year, my impassioned courtship began. Annemarie in Berlin helped me track down the Zürich publisher, Haffmans, and the artist in Cologne. I would have crawled on my knees through either city to have Der Rabe (the crow's name in German) on my cover, because he says exactly what *The Ravenous Muse* is about: eating books. Since you are here, you too must be a bibliogourmand, taking sensual as well as cerebral pleasure in the act of reading. And that's what's on the table here: creation caught in the act, writer and muse in flagrante delicto, biting each other's mouths.

The ravenous muse, ever eager to cultivate its tastes, comes in many moods and guises. Along with the hallu-cinogenic, the metaphysical, the provocative, and the capricious, you'll find the comic muse throughout, lightly and in darkness, with wit or macabre grin: dinner with the dead at the court of Versailles; a decapitation in Moscow that comes off thanks to a bottle of sunflower seed oil; a sardine can in Petersburg that's really a bomb; a fatal coffeepot chez Balzac. No mere messenger of inspiration, this muse is a sybarite, thinks of nothing but its own pleasure, demanding more and more—in its earthiest moments turning philosophical; at its loftiest, eating cake.

So what comes of all this reading, courting the crow, pleasing the muse? What's in it for you? Besides Olesha, Babel, Mandelstam, Mayakovsky, Chekhov, and Nabokov, you'll meet Dostoevsky out of his element— in the belly of a crocodile, an aspiring literary salon! Other authors you think you know may surprise you here: they've grown other voices and appetites, even biographies. If Flann O'Brien is new to you, then you may not realize how quickly food disappears from a table when a bicycle is nearby. In one library from Québec a rat saves the rarest volumes for himself, but is still a generous host, and when he has guests the air crackles, for his tastiest books are old. From France (like most books in that rat's library) come Flaubert, Roussel, Queneau, Roubaud, and Baudelaire the teenager swallowing a note in class.

Although *The Ravenous Muse* should be read in sequence for the full impact of its drama, you may flip ahead and read the note to "Devoured/Devouring" for one telling metaphor. Slavic Gastronomes ring so frequently for vodka and *zakuska* that they have their own chef, George Balanchine. Yolanta, misbehaving at their table in *The Red Shoes and Other Tattered Tales*, is sending a postcard here, also, and I've stolen pages from her contributions to *De Gustibus*, a doomed magazine that once enhanced oral gratification through epicurean uses of words. Although our paths cross and we share affinities, unlike Yolanta I do not wear baguettes on my feet, put my books in toasters, or ask for novels at the corner *boulangerie*.

It is always teatime, too, and who needs the Mad Hatter with Václav Havel, Osip Mandelstam, Paul Klee, and Milorad Pavić on the scene, each with his own teapot, brewing languages and dreams? If you happen by at the right moment, Emily Dickinson will give you candy, Lewis Carroll will tell you where to sit, and Ludwig Wittgenstein will wash the dishes, spellbound by the soap.

One last word about Der Rabe, the crow, who taunted me for years. As long as I was wooing and pursuing him (this is a love story, after all), the arrangement of this book eluded me. He was playing with my affections and testing my intent. Whenever my back was turned, in bored daylight, he would fly into the room, snatch up pages, and make off with them. More brazenly, at night (writing time for me), the crow would land in my hair, mocking me up with multiple confusions, then dive straight into the words—scattering and separating authors from titles, words from passages, translations from originals. He'd pause, eyeing me coquettishly from a shelf of my library, see if I was feeling thoroughly tortured, then zoom back to beat me with his wings and take words right out of my mouth, off my fingertips. However, once I had obtained permission for him to eat books on this book's cover, everything fell into place, and now you will find *your* place wherever your eye falls.

A manuscript is always a storm, worn to rags, torn by beaks.
—Osip Mandelstam

ℛ A Manicure with Mayakovsky

I was infatuated with Mayakovsky. I felt abashed whenever he appeared; I trembled whenever, and for whatever reason, his attention fell on me. . . . How happy I was when he praised me! I remember sitting in an actors' tavern, drinking wine and eating crayfish, and he was praising me for something, and I was on the very heights of happiness. Around us couples were dancing, and the girls were gazing over their shoulders at Mayakovsky, the two of us together, just the two of us—I was proud and exultant. . . . We were eating crayfish. When you remove their shells, you constantly prick your fingers on them, and Mayakovsky said to the head waiter,

"If only you'd given them a manicure or something."

—Yury Olesha, *No Day without a Line*

❧ Ice Cream and Lollipops in Cubist Paris

Pleasure chews and grinds us.

—Michel de Montaigne

❧ *It also licks us! See Gertrude Stein with her ice cream and The Princess Hoppy's shameless relatives at their "Orgy in the Screening Room."*

Toasted Susie is my ice cream.

—Gertrude Stein

That night for dessert we had a Singapore Ice Cream, which was studded with ginger and covered with whipped cream. Gertrude Stein looked very voluptuous as she licked at her spoon, which she did with half-closed eyes and a slow, stately rhythm. Her tongue suggested the bow of an expert fiddler who is playing a languid and delicious adagio.

—Frederic Prokosch, *Voices*

"We wanted to taste that special lollipop Picasso, Matisse, Miró, Apollinaire, Eluard, and Aragon had tasted and find out what it was like."

—Larry Rivers

ᠺ The Prodigious Appetite of Bicycles

—The behaviour of a bicycle with a very high content of homo sapiens, he explained, is very cunning and entirely remarkable. You never see them moving by themselves but you meet them in the least accountable of places unexpectedly. Did you ever see a bicycle leaning against the dresser in a warm kitchen when it is pouring outside?

—I did.

—Not very far from the fire?

—Yes.

—Near enough to the family to hear the conversation?

—I suppose so.

—Not a thousand miles from where they keep the eatables?

—I did not notice that. Good Lord, you do not mean to say that these bicycles eat *food?*

—They were never seen doing it, nobody ever caught
them with a mouthful of seedy cake. All I know is that
food disappears.

—What!

—It is not the first time I have noticed crumbs at the
front wheels of some of those gentlemen. . . .

—Nobody takes any notice, the Sergeant said softly.
Tom thinks that Pat is responsible for missing grub-
steaks, and Pat thinks that Tom is instrumental. Very
few of the people guess what is going on in such a fear-
somely infractional house.

—Flann O'Brien, *The Dalkey Archive*

ℛ Wolves and Bonbons

Is there not a sweet wolf within us
that demands its food?

—Emily Dickinson

Yes, there is, and it likes to eat between meals!

—Vučka Radulović

That wolf within us has many different hungers, and Emily Dickinson would indulge some of them among her smaller neighbors. Not always closing her door to the children, she would let them in for candy and cookies. On the more usual reclusive days, however, she would tie these goodies to a long string and lower them into the children's hands from her bedroom window.

This recalls depictions of Job in early Christian art, whose misery is delineated but also alleviated by the proximity of his wife, handing him a cake on the end of a stick.

Casserole Coiffure

 Raymond Roussel, whose methods for writing books were also extraordinary (and were explained in yet another literary tour de force, How I Wrote Certain of My Books), turned to crockery for his fine head of chestnut hair when his usual treatments were out of the question. Obsessed with the fear of its turning white, he was advised by a quack in France to sit under a hair dryer twice a week, which he did faithfully, nearly scorching his scalp. On arriving in Persia, with no electricity, he took to wearing hot casserole dishes on his head—and his gorgeous luster endured.

Fabulously wealthy, Roussel could indulge his gas-tronomic eccentricities, too. His Rolls-Royces traveled to do his shopping wherever the best regional products were to be had, and instead of having several meals a day, Roussel combined them into one, with sixteen different dishes, taking his time, of course, through a long darkness, between midnight and dawn.

Hunger and Hardship

25 January 1922

I've been neglecting my diary, which is a pity, since a lot of interesting things have been happening. [. . .] I am still without a job. My wife and I are eating very badly, which is why I don't feel like writing. Black bread costs 20 thousand a pound.

26 January 1922

I have joined an itinerant group of actors; we're going to perform in the suburbs. They pay 125 a performance, which is appallingly little. And of course there will be no time to write because of these performances. It's a vicious circle. My wife and I are half-starving.

9 February 1922

This is the blackest period of my life. My wife and I are starving. I have had to accept a little flour, vegetable oil and some potatoes from my uncle. [. . .] I have run all over Moscow, but there are no jobs. My felt boots have fallen apart.

—Mikhail Bulgakov

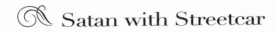# Satan with Streetcar

In Mikhail Bulgakov's The Master and Margarita, *the unfortunate accident uncannily predicted by the unearthly, unholy foreigner at Moscow's Patriarch's Ponds stars a bottle of sunflower seed oil and a beautiful streetcar conductor. Without the sunflower seed oil, Berlioz would never have slipped and lost his head—literally, for it bounces across the cobblestones without him.*

Although he was standing in safety, the cautious Berlioz decided to retreat behind the railing. He put his hand on the turnstile and took a step backward. He missed his grip and his foot slipped on the cobblestones as inexorably as though on ice. As it slid toward the trolley tracks, his other leg gave way and Berlioz was thrown across the track. Grabbing wildly, Berlioz fell prone. He struck his head violently on the cobblestones and the gilded moon flashed hazily across his vision. He had just time to turn on his back, drawing his legs up to his stomach with a frenzied movement, and as he turned over he saw the woman trolley car driver's face, white with horror above her red necktie, as she bore down on him with irresistible force and speed. . . .

Enter shortly a walk-on woman who explains the accident:

"Anna, it was our Anna! . . . She was carrying a quart of sunflower-seed oil to the grocery and she broke her jug on the turnstile! It went all over her skirt and ruined it, and she swore and swore! And that poor man must have slipped on the oil and fallen under the car. . . ."

His head and body communing at the coroner's, Berlioz's apartment is instantly coveted, and the letters of supplication pour in, a most winsome one of interest to our muse:

They contained entreaties, threats, intrigue, denunciations, promises to redecorate the apartment, remarks about overcrowding and the impossibility of sharing an apartment with hoodlums. Among them was a description, shattering in its literary power, of the theft of some meatballs from someone's jacket pocket in apartment No. 31, two threats of suicide and one confession of secret pregnancy.

*But wait! Just because Berlioz is gone by Chapter Four
doesn't mean we can't go back and find him when he was
still alive. In the second sentence of Chapter One, we
learn that the literary editor Berlioz is well fed; he even
carries "his decorous hat by the brim as though it were a
cake." Bulgakov sets a comical tone with the help of
some apricots. Berlioz and Bezdomny want lemonade or
beer from the kiosk at Patriarch's Ponds, but the only
drink to be had is some warm apricot juice:*

The apricot juice produced a rich yellow froth, making
the air smell like a hairdresser's. After drinking it the
two writers immediately began to hiccup.

*As the two men sit down and continue their conversation,
Berlioz suddenly stops hiccuping and has some conster-
nating physical sensations followed by an urge to run
away—before meeting up with his macabre doom, Pon-
tius Pilate, and the devil who arranges it all (after
telling them about having breakfast with Kant and other
implausibilities that have the men as confounded as the
heroes of* The Dalkey Archive *in a similar beginning and
meeting). Bezdomny, however, continues to hiccup
throughout this chapter, and Bulgakov knows just when
to make him do so, as the conversation veers from the
pompous to the impertinent to the fantastic.*

The Master and Margarita *features a trinity of diabol-ical intent, the most fascinating (for the book's charac-ters as well as its readers) being a huge black cat—one of the most alluringly wicked and rakish figures you'll ever meet—"the size of a pig, black as soot and with luxuri-ant cavalry officer's whiskers"—who is often seen trot-ting or walking on its hind legs. When Berlioz's flatmate discovers him ensconced in their apartment (the reason Berlioz had to die), it is in the pose of a sybarite: "a black cat of revolting proportions sprawled in a noncha-lant attitude on the pouf, a glass of vodka in one paw and a fork, on which he had just speared a pickled mush-room, in the other."*

Vladimir Nabokov also liked to go about such things comfortably: "I like to eat and drink in a recumbent posi-tion (preferably on a couch)," he writes in Speak, Mem-ory. *The cat and Nabokov would approve of Bernard Rudofsky's* Now I Lay Me Down to Eat, *a sustained refu-tation of the chair and other upright positions, discom-forts of our civilized society. Rudofsky shows how wrong are most paintings of the Last Supper: in keeping with the customs of the time, Christ and his disciples would have been diagonally horizontal—that is, propped up on an elbow, and definitely not in straight-backed chairs.*

Now I don't want to give away too much of the story—but Berlioz's head does return to it: the skull is used as a goblet (emerald eyes, pearl teeth, top of skull opening with a hinge) for a gruesome cocktail the night of the demonic ball in the chapter "Satan's Rout." During the final hours in the expropriated apartment, the cat has a shoot-out with the Moscow authorities, plays mortally wounded, and revives himself with a slug of kerosene. His taste throughout the book runs definitely to zakuska—we see him salting and peppering a slice of pineapple, chasing it down with spirits, smearing an oyster with mustard. You may also meet the cat again, in evening dress and playing with Neptune's mouth, when you come to the "Night of Infernal Debauch."

 Ain't Misbehavin'

I mingled among the other guests, clucking appreciatively at their hoary anecdotes, splaying my fingers in mock protestation, dilating my pupils in genuine horror, owning the verity of each proffered compliment; and if the smallest indecency poked its snout through the muddle of some gentleman's monologue, I would hasten to compose my features into a picture of doelike innocence before bounding off into a bowl of punch.

—Cinderella

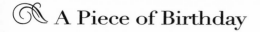 A Piece of Birthday

Such birthday felicities had never befallen her! But on the eve of her fiftieth year, friends frocked from far and wide to toast her cockles, with her some better ones, turn her over to the rosy hands of dawn. They festooned her with pork butts and sackbuts, rounded off the evening and their profiles with sacher torte, and kept the jereboams foaming at the mouths they opened to them, when they weren't plastering their kissers on the honored guest's.

—Tamara Chagrinsky

Magritte and the Mauled Dutch Cheese

One day, Belgian Surrealist painter René Magritte entered a grocery store and asked to buy some Dutch cheese. The shopkeeper grabbed the round in the window, but he protested, saying he wanted his piece cut from a different round of the same kind. She asked why: after all the cheese was identical. "No, madame," Magritte replied, "the one in the window has been looked at all day by people passing by."

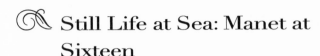 Still Life at Sea: Manet at Sixteen

*Like every young man of his time, Manet was nearly
forced to study law. Somehow, he got his father to relent,
but then he had to offer an alternative. "I want to be a
sailor," he said, little knowing that artistic opportunities
awaited him in the ship's larder. The experience is on a
smaller scale, yet is not unlike the way Christo got
started: put to work at simulation by the Bulgarian government to make the farms appear more picturesque, the
laborers' lives more idyllic.*

At sixteen, young Manet signed on board the *Le Havre
et Guadeloupe* and headed out on a six-month voyage
to Rio de Janeiro. He spent much of his time at sea in
sketching, and the indulgent captain contributed to his
artistic education only by asking him to repaint the red
skins on a supply of Dutch cheeses that showed signs
of going bad.

—Otto Friedrich,
Olympia: Paris in the Age of Manet

A Cup of Accommodation

A white cup means a wedding. A wet cup means a vacation. A strong cup means an especial regulation. A single cup means a capital arrangement between the drawer and the place that is open.

—Gertrude Stein, *Tender Buttons*

Tea and Alchemy

My happiest moment is when I prepare a glass of hot, strong tea, and then sit down with it to read, think or write a letter. I've become a fanatical devotee of Earl Grey, which in England, as everyone knows, is consumed only by little old ladies during afternoon tea parties, and which the English tea lover scorns as a perfumed, old-maidenish drink.

—Václav Havel, *Letters to Olga*

Dream: I asked the geishas only for a little music and some "of the tea that serves as a manifold substitute for all the geishas of the world."

At the slightest temptation I heard a soft knocking. When I followed the knocking, a small sprite stretched out his tiny hand toward me and led me gently upward into his region.

There, things fell up, not down. A light breakfast, including eggs, was appetizingly laid out on the ceiling.

—Paul Klee, *Diaries*

"A stranger appeared out of the desert," they said, "but he's good with a shovel." They gave him tea, sugar, and a spoon, although it had a hole in it and its handle was twisted, as if somebody had tried by brute force to wring something out of it, a tear, a drop of tea or butterfat. In short, he warmed himself by the stove, sipped his tea, and was flabbergasted. It was the famous white tea that used to be sold in tsarist Russia for ten silver rubles a pound; dogs given the tea became so rabid that they tore to pieces everything they could get hold of.

—Milorad Pavić, *Landscape Painted with Tea*

⚸ Beyond the Bliny

In the days when I didn't know people were reading
and judging me, I wrote serenely, as if eating *bliny;*
now I'm afraid when I write.

—Anton Chekhov

⚸ *Now this is a funny case of two sensibilities sharing the*
same tastes across the century and the sprawl of Europe. I
know just how Chekhov felt, although as usual I've
turned things around. My plans for this book had in-
cluded long hours at the Bibliothèque Nationale, and I
went to considerable trouble to reverse my nocturnal
hours so I would arrive in the morning for the scholarly
stampede, then the three-hour wait for a coveted volume
of the Bongoût brothers or la Cheminée grignotée *by*
Sanglier de Rostoff. But before I could make much
progress in my research, I was banished from the rarefied
atmosphere forever (well, truthfully, for nine months, to
be followed by a probation period on location, hands off
certain books quand même) *for one mere ravenous misbe-*
havior. Of my offense, I can only say I had no idea I was
up to such antics; the damage, however, was done. Bend-
ing over my studies, a small stack of memoirs en voyage
(mostly Middle Eastern and Georgian, Ukrainian, Tran-

sylvanian—did you know that there's a strong Armenian influence in the latter cuisine?), I was calmly inserting bliny *in between pages—to mark my place? or did I not distinguish between the pages and my lunch? Whatever the reason, I lost both my lunch and my place, as I was hustled out, my bliny and notebooks thrown after me into the courtyard for cigarettes.*

I went off and cried into a bowl of pelmeyni *at one of my favorite Caspian cafés near St. Alexandre Nevsky Cathedral, about which I also have a confession to make, from an earlier year.*

Having read of the church and its neighborhood near Parc Monceau, I set out to explore them, paw the books, gaze at the icons, admire the samovars. But as I walked down the side of rue Daru lined with tearooms and restaurants, my eyes were eating up their windows, absorbing the words on menus posted at the doors. Popping into a lavish establishment on the corner to inquire about the hours and make off with a card, but really just to look the place over, I asked the proprietor if he could tell me where the church was. "It's right across the street," he said, pointing that way through the window, "isn't it big enough for you?" (for it was an immense and gilded glory, set back to command all views). "Oh, I was so taken with all the zakuska *in the windows, I was blinded!" I said, assuring him of my return.*

Sergei, as I soon learned he was called, and I enjoyed

the beginnings of a flirtatious friendship that came to a sudden halt when he realized that far from having a roaring appetite for his restaurant and the hours of conversation at its tables, I was interested in merely looking at the zakuska *and reading about them—and even there I preferred these Russian dishes and ingredients as imagery, comparisons, such as those in which Nikolai Gogol excelled. A rival to his flair for edible words has not materialized. Gogol wrote some of the best-fed books of all time, and yet he was systematically starved to death after he fed the rest of* Dead Souls *to the fire. But the gruesome end came after his years of wandering in Italy, Germany, Austria, and France. He settled in Rome, where he ate without restraint: restaurants were temples to him; waiters, priests. From there, he returned to Russia in shattered health, but also with Parmesan in his pockets, and he prepared pasta, with brio, for his friends.*

After indulging his appetites all over Europe, Gogol in Russia switched religions from those epicurean devotions he so enjoyed in Rome. He fell under the sway of a fanatical Orthodox priest, Father Matthew, who filled his mind with the horrors that awaited him in hell. Those horrors then arrived in life, with three sets of doctors applying their bizarre methods simultaneously while Gogol wasted away on nothing but several spoonfuls of watery oatmeal soup or sauerkraut brine per day. Mustard plasters on his back, leeches clinging to his nose and mouth, biting liquids dripped on his head, Gogol (this freezes and braises the marrow of our muse's bones) was alternately plunged into ice-cold baths and surrounded by steaming hot loaves of freshly baked bread.

In "The Tale of How Ivan Ivanovich Quarreled with Ivan Nikiforovich," Gogol delineates his antagonists' characters through similes and behavior composed of food:

Ivan Ivanovich's head is like a radish, tail downwards; Ivan Nikiforovich's head is like a radish, tail upwards. . . . Ivan Ivanovich is very angry if a fly gets into his borscht: he is quite beside himself then—he will throw the plate and his host is sure to catch hell! Ivan Nikiforovich is exceedingly fond of bathing and, when he is sitting up to his neck in water, he orders the table and samovar to be set in the water, too, and is very fond of drinking tea in such refreshing coolness. . . .

Even before he's gotten very far with them, Gogol mentions in passing a woman named Agafya Fedoseevna, who'd bitten off the tax assessor's ear. Mouths have a great deal more than dialogue to tend to in any of Gogol's works.

As the dispute between these two friends, Ivan and

Ivan, reaches the Mirogorod District Court and Gogol is
singing the splendors of this finest building in the dis-
trict, with its eight windows looking out over the central
square and its pool, he relates an unusual gastronomic
theft that's left its mark on the roof:

It is the only one painted the color of granite; all the
other houses in Mirogorod are simply whitewashed. Its
roof is all made of wood, and would, indeed, have been
painted red, if the oil intended for that purpose had
not been eaten by the office clerks with onions, for, as
luck would have it, it was Lent, and so the roof was left
unpainted.

Plat du Jour and *Zakuska* for Petrouchka

I'm not so excited or hungry to tell people something.
What I must do is supply my restaurant with a plat du
jour. I have to "feed" people because we charge them
money. They come and pay $2.95 or $3.95, whatever it
is, and we have to give them something to look at.
That's my job. So I never know ahead of time what I'm

going to do. I have to calculate. If I've already given them something American, something modern, or something Russian, like Tchaikovsky or Rimsky-Korsakov or Stravinsky, then I may decide that I must have something French, either old or modern. Or maybe it should be an English or a Japanese ballet. I do something like that. You have to calculate your menu. Like planning a meal, you have to have this and this and that.

—George Balanchine

How Balanchine Got Igor Stravinsky Out of a Difficult Mood

Stravinsky loved to eat, and drink vodka, so when he was being difficult, Balanchine would start talking to him about these lovely things he was going to fix him—with sour cream . . . and Stravinsky would come right out of it, for Balanchine was a wonderful cook. Ten days before Stravinsky died, Balanchine went to see him and started telling him of the zakuska he'd bring him, Stravinsky's interest was aroused, and he said only one word—screaming—"WHEN?"

Bread of the Night

Some ask that poetry be relieved of her armor; their wound is sick of an eternity of tweezers. But walking naked on her feet of reeds, her feet of pebbles, she lets herself be nowhere confined. Woman! On her mouth we kiss the madness of time; or side by side with the zenith cricket, she sings through the winter night in the bakery of the poor, under the softness of a loaf of light.

—René Char, *Leaves of Hypnos*

Atanas slept in that bed when he was a boy and every evening waited for me to come and comb his hair before going to sleep. He could not fall asleep uncombed. I would wet his head and knead it at length, like dough. And then, I remember, I would slice his hair with a comb, as though with a knife, and divide his hair the way one divides a loaf of bread. Finally, I would kiss him, stir the fire in the room, and tell him that by morning his hair would rise like dough for fritters. . . .

—Milorad Pavić

In Landscape Painted with Tea, *quoted above, bread is mentioned in so many different contexts that it nearly achieves the status of a character. Salt occurs with similar frequency and effect, so that you begin to know what bread and salt are all about, and along with them, the qualities and destinies of those who consume them, whose experiences are described in their terms. Food is, too, a witness to all that is thought, said, and felt. The bread seems to hear the words not spoken, even, it is so present, attentive, alive. A crowded church is "as full as a spoon."*

A book by Pavić weaves a spell of literary, historical, linguistic, religious erudition, and yet you can eat every page. Bringing our mouths and bellies to attention, Pavić dances his ambiguities and mystery across our senses, while refilling our cups and plates. It turns out this is how to engage the mind, keeping the body present, content, and desirous—never sated: very important!—for that's the nature of the ravenous muse, to go on wanting, to demand new combinations and subtleties for the tongue that both tastes and talks.

In the Mirror of Our Dreams

A recipe concocted by Leonora Carrington and Remedios Varo, and recorded in Varo's notebook, in the course of their pseudoscientific investigations, this one to stimulate erotic dreams, calls for the following:

a kilo of horseradish, three white hens, a head of garlic, four kilos of honey, a mirror, two calf livers, a brick, two clothespins, a corset with stays, two false mustaches, and hats to taste.

These are the instructions for preparing the cook:

Put on the corset and make it quite tight. Sit down in front of the mirror, relax your nervous tension, smile and try on the mustaches and hats according to your taste (three-cornered, Napoleonic, cardinal's hat, imitation with lace, Basque beret, etc.). . . . Run and pour the broth (which should be very reduced) quickly into a cup. Quickly come back with it to in front of the mirror; smile, take a sip of broth, try on one of the mustaches, take another sip, try on a hat, drink, try on everything, taking sips in between and do it all as quickly as you can.

—Janet A. Kaplan, *Unexpected Journeys*

I have tried this on many occasions, and am pleased to offer you this report.

The only corset available, in my family's attic, belonged to my great-grandmother, and it transported me to the Zillertal, where I fell in love with a slim young cowherd named Wolfie, whom I enjoyed in many outdoor settings not far from the cows. These dreams helped bring me to terms with the cowboy obsession I've had since the age of two, and will no doubt inspire me to write, at last, the first country 'n' western hit in Tyrolean dialect.

I found that by wearing my real-life lover's hat, I would dream of myself as if I were he, his true feelings uncensored, unadorned, unmolested by inapt words—which only deepened mine for him (they had already been repeatedly heightened by our many walks to the top of the Panthéon). So now, on special occasions, we switch hats and sleep, and wake up with knowing looks on the other side of ourselves.

If you substitute a crow for one of the hens, the brick will immediately turn into a book—and that book will contain the urgent message that's been evading you all these years. But you have to sleep on it first.

ᴄᴀ Rippling Muscles of Porridge

Judith had crossed the muck and rabble of the yard, and now entered the house by the back door.

In the large kitchen, which occupied most of the middle of the house, a sullen fire burned, the smoke of which wavered up the blackened walls and over the deal table, darkened by age and dirt, which was roughly set for a meal. A snood full of coarse porridge hung over the fire, and standing with one arm resting upon the high mantel, looking moodily down into the heaving contents of the snood, was a tall young man whose riding-boots were splashed with mud to the thigh, and whose coarse linen shirt was open to his waist. The firelight lit up his diaphragm muscles as they heaved slowly in rough rhythm with the porridge.

He looked up as Judith entered, and gave a short, defiant laugh, but said nothing. Judith slowly crossed over until she stood by his side. She was as tall as he. They stood in silence, she staring at him, and he down into the secret crevasses of the porridge.

"Well, mother mine," he said at last, "here I am, you see. I said I would be in time for breakfast, and I have kept my word."

His voice had a low, throaty, animal quality, a sneering warmth that wound a velvet ribbon of sexuality over the outward coarseness of the man.

Judith's breath came in long shudders. She thrust her arms deeper into her shawl. The porridge gave an ominous, leering heave; it might almost have been endowed with life, so uncannily did its movements keep pace with the human passions that throbbed above it.

"Cur," said Judith, levelly, at last. "Coward! Liar! Libertine! Who were you with last night? . . . Seth—my son . . ." Her deep, dry voice quivered, but she whipped it back, and her next words flew out at him like a lash.

"Do you want to break my heart?"

"Yes," said Seth, with an elemental simplicity.

The porridge boiled over.

Judith knelt, and hastily and absently ladled it off the floor back into the snood, biting back her tears.

—Stella Gibbons, *Cold Comfort Farm*

❦ Stretch It Out, Mr. Twemlow, and That Sad Café

❦ *Charles Dickens's* Our Mutual Friend *features a family relation who is often eaten upon:*

There was an innocent piece of dinner-furniture that went upon easy castors and was kept over a livery stable-yard in Duke Street, Saint James's, when not in use. . . . The name of this article was Twemlow. Being first cousin to Lord Snigsworth, he was in frequent requisition, and at many houses might be said to represent the dining-table in its normal state. Mr. and Mrs. Veneering, for example, arranging a dinner, habitually started with Twemlow, and then put leaves in him, or added guests to him. Sometimes, the table consisted of Twemlow and half a dozen leaves; sometimes, of Twemlow and a dozen leaves; sometimes, Twemlow was pulled out to his utmost extent of twenty leaves.

—Charles Dickens

To help with his father's debts, the twelve-year-old Dickens had to work in a wax factory. In nearby Saint Martin's Lane was a café the door of which had a glass oval plaque painted with the word CAFE. Later in his life, whenever he found himself inside a café, however different otherwise but with an inscribed glass sign, he would always read it backwards, EFAC, as in his gloomiest reveries—and the sight would chill his blood.

ℛ A Puzzle of Pancakes

ℛ *Pancakes are a far cry from bliny,* but they take quite a*
fanciful turn in Flann O'Brien's novel The Third Policeman, *which you might turn to if "The Prodigious Ap-*
petite of Bicycles" intrigues you. The Third Policeman, *a*
sort of hell on wheels, includes one Sergeant Mac-
Cruiskeen, for whom the pancake, in various phrasings
and extremes, expresses his bewilderment as each intellec-
tual challenge or unanswerable question arises. Among
these variations you will find:

"It is a difficult pancake," MacCruiskeen said, "a
very compound crux."

"It is one of the most compressed and intricate
pancakes I have ever known."

"That is the supreme pancake," he said. "If you
could say what the shouts mean, that could be the mak-
ings of the answer."

"You will agree," he said, "that it is a fascinating

---

* Geographically and culturally, and they are sadly strangers to sour
cream and caviar, the usual bliny accomplices. Sad, too, is the scene
in *Tess of the d'Urbervilles*, when Tess, on the road of tribulations
as an agricultural laborer, takes out her lunch: a solitary pancake.

pancake and a conundrum of great incontinence, a
phenomenon of the first rarity."

*⫝ I'm not withholding the exchanges in which these pan-
cakes occur just to tease you; the world of* The Third Policeman *is so absurd, and the conversations within it, that
they need the full story for you* to *follow them with total
disbelief, exercising your mental bicycles on the surface of
a nightmare.*

⫝ Blancmange with Erik Satie

A Musician's Day

An artist must regulate his life. Here is my precise
daily schedule. I rise at 7:18; am inspired from 10:30 to
11:47. I lunch at 12:11 and leave the table at 12:14. A
healthy horse-back ride on my property from 1:19 to
2:35. Another round of inspiration from 3:12 to 4:07.

From 5:00 to 6:47 various occupations (fencing, re-
flection, immobility, visits, contemplation, dexterity,
swimming, etc.)

Dinner is served at 7:16 and finished at 7:20. After-
ward from 8:09 to 9:59 symphonic readings out loud.

I go to bed regularly at 10:37. Once a week I wake up with a start at 3:14 A.M. (Tuesdays).

I eat only white foods: eggs, sugar, shredded bones, the fat of dead animals, rice, turnips, sausages in camphor, pastry, cheese (the white varieties), cotton salad, and certain kinds of fish (skinned).

I boil my wine and drink it cold mixed with fushsia juice. I have a good appetite but never talk when eating for fear of strangling.

I breathe carefully (a little at a time) and dance very rarely. When walking I hold my sides and look steadily behind me.

Being of serious demeanor, it is unintentional when I laugh. I always apologize very affably.

I sleep with only one eye closed; I sleep very hard. My bed is round with a hole in it for my head to go through. Every hour a servant takes my temperature and gives me another.

For a long time I have subscribed to a fashion magazine. I wear a white cap, white socks, and a white vest.

My doctor has always told me to smoke. He even explains himself: "Smoke, my friend. Otherwise someone else will smoke in your place."

—Erik Satie, *Mémoires d'un amnésique*
from *The Banquet Years,* Roger Shattuck

The Bear in His Milk Pans, a Ballet in an Icebox

As for this business of my moving at once to Paris, we'll have to put it off, or rather settle it here and now. This is *impossible* for me now . . . I know myself well enough, and it would mean losing a whole winter, and perhaps the whole book. Bouilhet can talk: he's happy writing anywhere; he's been working away for a dozen years despite continual disturbances . . . But I am like a row of milk pans: if you want the cream to form, you have to leave them exactly where they are.

—Gustave Flaubert

What I think is that you have to use everything life gives you—like opening an icebox and reaching inside—and you use it well and modestly and hope that you're a little better at it than you were yesterday. Since you are being judged by an audience, you must supply them, not with a fantastic dinner every day, but sometimes with a glass of milk.

—George Balanchine

Ghazels and Lamb Chops with Ghālib

Chishti Sahib was a dapper-looking man. From his moderate demeanor no one would have guessed at all the pedagogical frenzy he carried on his back, as densely packed as the hump of a camel. I do not even think he was fully aware of it himself, so at this moment he would probably be most put out of step to know that, if we could meet him, both Shahid and I would take his hand in celebration, saying, "You have changed my life." Chishti was the last in a long line of Urdu tutors who straggled into the house to teach us Urdu; some of them were very peculiar people, and I do not recall doing much learning until Chishti came our way. For Chishti gave us the ghazel. Until that time we had only perfunctory acquaintance with that rare breed of poem, conceiving of it as the kind of writing that someone like my father would resort to when he was in his most declarative mood. But Chishti changed that for us, filling our brains with a mathematical inge-nuity that felt heady as incense. "It's like geometry—no, it's relativity," we breathed, in wonder that our faulty discourse had not noticed this before. Chishti's face would transform at the thought of a verse, and we, spellbound, could only follow the lineaments of his ex-pression as it coaxed us in precarious veers up to the vertiginous idiom of Mirzā Asadullāh Khān Ghālib. That master poet of Delhi wrote at the court of the last Mughal emperor and, after the Mutiny of 1857, mourned fiercely for the demise of the city he had known. Mirzā Sahib, my salaam to you.

I did, in recent days, pay my respects to Ghālib, stopping in at the Ghālib Academy in the Nizamuddin section of Delhi. Upstairs in the academy there is a library and a museum: it soothed me to be there, laying a finger on those old spines, bending over those faded letters. Then, to my surprise, I noticed that half the museum was given over to an exhibition called "The Foods Ghālib Liked to Eat." That musty glass case had obviously been there for years, with its array of wax mangoes, and chicken stuffed with saffron, and even a lamb chop. "What an amazing idea," I thought, "what a wonderful thing to do for a poet!" Ghālib, a mischievous man, would have been amused, I felt sure; but I also felt sure that I had hit upon the perfect present for Shahid. One year, for his birthday, I could just give him a glass box entitled "Foods That Ghālib Liked to Eat." It would rapidly assume pride of place, I know, in that boy's gypsy home.

—Sara Suleri, *Meatless Days*

☙ Dining with the Dead at the Court of Versailles

☙ *Monsieur Le Prince, Henri-Jules de Bourbon, duc d'Enghien, in the court of Louis XIV, attacked by fever and gout repeatedly in his later years, caused his doctor great distress, especially when he refused to eat, claiming that he was already dead, and that the dead did not eat.*

Yet if he had not eaten, he would have died for a fact. But he could never be persuaded that he was alive, and consequently, that he should eat. Finally Finot and another doctor who attended him decided to agree that he was dead, but to argue that some dead persons ate. They offered to show him some, and brought in several persons they could count on, and who said they were as dead as he was but still went on eating. This device did the trick, but he would only eat with the other "dead" and Finot. His appetite was good, although Finot despaired at the persistence of his fantasy. Finot would double up with laughter, however, when recounting the otherworldly conversations that took place at these meals.

—The Duc de Saint-Simon, *The Age of Magnificence*

Watermelon on Wheels along the Road of Dead Souls

At the other end of town there was happening something that was to make our hero's plight even worse. To wit: through remote streets and by-alleys of the town rumbled a most queer vehicle. . . . It looked neither like a *tarantas,* nor like a calash, nor like a *britzka,* being in sooth more like a fat-cheeked very round watermelon set upon wheels. The cheeks of this melon, that is, the carriage doors, that bore remnants of their former yellow varnish, closed very poorly owing to the bad state of the handles and locks which had been perfunctorily fixed up by means of string. The melon was filled with chintz cushions, small ones, long ones, and ordinary ones, and stuffed with bags containing loaves of bread and such eatables as *kalachi* [purse-shaped rolls], *kokoorki* [buns with egg or cheese stuffing], *skorodoomki* [skoro-dumplings] and *krendels* [a sort of magnified *kalach* in the form of a capital B, richly flavored and decorated]. A chicken-pie and a *rassolnik* [a sophisticated giblet-pie] were visible even on the top of the carriage.

—Nikolai Gogol,
Dead Souls (with Vladimir Nabokov
translating and enlightening)

The *Kalatch* according to Mandelstam

—Where are we going? I asked an old woman in a gypsy shawl.

—To the city of Malinov, she replied, but with such aching melancholy that my heart contracted with an evil forboding.

The old woman, rummaging about in her striped bundle, took out some table silver, a cloth, and velvet slippers.

The threadbare wedding carriages crawled on and on, reeling like contrabasses. . . .

—Look, exclaimed someone, sticking his head out of the window. There is Malinov already.

But there was no city there. Instead, growing right in the snow were some large, warty raspberries.

—But that's a raspberry patch, I gasped, beside myself with joy, and began to run with the others, filling my shoes with snow. My shoe came untied and because of that I was seized with a feeling of great guilt and disorder.

And they led me into a hateful Warsaw room and made me drink water and eat onion.

I kept bending over to tie my shoe with a double knot and put everything in its proper order—but in vain. It was impossible to recoup anything or repair anything: everything went backwards, as always happens in a dream. . . .

Are you familiar with this condition? When it's just as if every object were running a fever, when they are all joyously excited and ill: barriers in the street, posters shedding their skin, grand pianos thronging at the depot like an intelligent, leaderless herd, born for frenzies of the sonata and for boiled water. . . .

Then, I confess, I am unable to endure the quarantine, and, smashing thermometers, through the contagious labyrinth I boldly stride, behung with subordinate clauses like happy bargain buys . . . and into the waiting sack fly the crisp pastry birds, naive as the plastic art of the first centuries of Christianity, and the *kalatch*, the common *kalatch*, no longer conceals from me that it was conceived by the baker as a Russian lyre of voiceless dough.

—Osip Mandelstam, *The Egyptian Stamp*

Chekhov on a Tray

His dictionary is poor, his combination of words almost trivial—the purple patch, the juicy verb, the hothouse adjective, the crème-de-menthe epithet, brought in on a silver tray, these were foreign to him.

— Vladimir Nabokov, on Chekhov

In the Boxcar with Anton Chekhov

Chekhov was far from home, with his wife, Olga, in Badenweiler, Germany, when he died of consumption. At the Villa Friederike, on July 2, 1904, his doctor had a bottle of champagne brought to the writer. Chekhov, accepting the glass offered to him, said, "It's been such a long time since I drank champagne," and, emptying the glass, lay on his side and took his final breaths. A long journey back to Russia was inevitable.

Before leaving Badenweiler, Olga arranged for the remains to be transported to Moscow, where the burial was to take place on July 9. That day a group of friends gathered at the station to meet the train carrying the body. They were flabbergasted to learn that his coffin had traveled in a dirty green van* with the words FOR OYSTERS written in large letters on the door.

Gorky was furious. "I feel like screaming, weeping, brawling with indignation and wrath," he wrote to his wife.† He knew that Chekhov would not have cared whether his body traveled in a basket of dirty laundry.

—Henri Troyat, *Chekhov*

* My friend the Palestinian author Soraya Antonius suggests that it must have been a chilled car, and they were taking care of the body, not humiliating the man. I would also add that oysters are ever the perfect accompaniment to champagne, and Chekhov's final meal was now complete.

† Gorky's reaction must be taken with a grain of salt (from his own tears): Nina Berberova describes in her memoirs how Gorky used to cry copiously over his own fresh pages, smearing the ink as he wrote.

☙ Grandfather (While She Whips Her Cream)

A man named Armando, born in the town of Salitre on the coast of Ecuador, presented me with the story of his grandfather.

The great grandchildren took turns looking after him. They had put a padlock and chain on the door. Don Segundo Hidalgo said that was the cause of his ailments:

"I have the rheumatism of a castrated cat."

At the age of a hundred, Don Segundo would take advantage of any carelessness to mount his horse bareback and slip out in search of girlfriends. No one knew as much about women and horses. He had populated the town of Salitre and its surroundings, since becoming a father for the first time at thirteen.

The grandfather confessed to having had three hundred women, although everyone knew he'd had over four hundred. But one of them, Blanquita, had been the womanliest woman of them all.

It had been thirty years since Blanquita died and he still invoked her name every day at dusk. Armando, the grandson who told me this story, would hide and spy upon the secret ceremony. On the balcony, illuminated by the dying light, the grandfather would open an antique powder box, a round box with pink angels on the lid, and bring the powder puff to his nose.

"I believe I know you," he would murmur, inhaling the faint perfume of the powder, *"I believe I know you."*

And he would rock himself very gently, murmuring as he dozed off in the rocking chair.

Every evening, the grandfather would perform his homage to the woman he loved the most, and once a week he would betray her. He was unfaithful with a fat lady who prepared extremely complicated dishes on television. The grandfather, owner of the first and only television in the town of Salitre, would never miss the program. He would bathe, shower, and dress entirely in white, as if for a party, putting on his best hat, patent leather boots, a vest with golden buttons and silk necktie, and would sit right in front of the screen. While the fat lady whipped her cream and wielded her ladle, explaining the keys to some unique, exclusive, incomparable flavor, the grandfather would leer at her and blow her furtive kisses. His bank savings book poked out of the breast pocket of his suit. The grandfather placed the book that way as if carelessly, so the fat lady would see he was no poor ragamuffin.

—Eduardo Galeano, *The Book of Embraces*

Music, Memory, and Mandelstam

Musical notation caresses the eye no less than music itself soothes the ear. The blacks of the piano scale climb up and down like lamplighters. Each measure is a little boat loaded with raisins and black grapes. . . .

The grand piano is an intelligent and good-natured house animal with fibrous, wooden flesh, golden veins, and eternally inflamed bone. We protected it from catching a cold and nourished it with sonatinas, light as asparagus.

—Osip Mandelstam, *The Egyptian Stamp*

No matter when I'd drop by, Mrs Mandelstam would insist that I have something to sustain me—tea and jam; sometimes a cup of cabbage soup, schi, or a little bread and cheese. Once we shared a bottle of Asti Spumante, a gift from an admirer of her husband's poetry. Asti had been one of Mandelstam's favorite wines.

I will never forget that evening, spent in the tiny maid's room which served as her Moscow headquarters during that particular visit. There was only an iron

bed, on which she half reclined, a chair, and a suitcase
which served as a table, and on which stood a Persian
copper bird that Mandelstam had loved, one of the few
possessions Mrs Mandelstam had been able to save.
With the wine we had two hothouse tomatoes, which
someone had sent from Georgia to her hosts, and caviar
which I had brought from the Metropole. As we ate and
drank, she recited dozens of her husband's poems,
some of them unknown to me, since none of his works
had been published anywhere during the last years of
his life. It was a moving feast in memory of a great
poet.

—Olga Carlisle, "Festive Tables in Russia"

 Salon

Madame Aubernon, however, a somewhat vulgar aristo-
crat of the old school, passionately interested in literature and the theater, conducted her rival *salon* like a
lion tamer. About a dozen guests attended her poorly
cooked dinners in the Rue d'Astorg, and Madame
Aubernon alone decided the subject for discussion.
One guest at a time was permitted to orate, and his
chances of a second invitation depended on the bril-
liance of his performance. The hostess silenced any
disorderly interruption by ringing a little porcelain bell
which stood at her right hand. One evening when
Renan was discoursing at some length, she had several
times to call to order the dramatist Labiche (author of
The Italian Straw Hat). When she finally asked him to
speak, he admitted with some reluctance that he had
only wanted to ask for more peas. On another occasion
Madame Aubernon asked D'Annunzio point-blank
what he thought of love; his reply was not designed to
bring him a second invitation: "Read my books,
Madame, and let me eat my dinner." A lady, asked with
similar abruptness to speak her piece on the subject of
adultery, replied, "You must pardon me, Madame. For
this evening I prepared incest."

—Roger Shattuck, *The Banquet Years*

Dostoevsky's Crocodile

And it was at that moment that a terrible, I may say un-
natural, scream set the room vibrating. Not knowing
what to think, for the first moment I stood still, numb
with horror, but noticing that Elena Ivanovna was
screaming too, I quickly turned round—and what did I
behold! I saw—oh heavens!—I saw the luckless Ivan
Matveitch in the terrible jaws of the crocodile, held by
them round the waist, lifted horizontally in the air and
desperately kicking. Then—one moment and no trace
remained of him. But I must describe it in detail, for I
stood all the while motionless, and had time to watch
the whole process taking place before me with an attention and interest such as I never remember to have felt
before. . . .

The crocodile began by turning the unhappy Ivan
Matveitch in his terrible jaws so that he could swallow
his legs first; then bringing up Ivan Matveitch, who
kept trying to jump out and clutching at the sides of
the tank, sucked him down again as far as his waist.
Then bringing him up again, gulped him down, and so
again and again. In this way Ivan Matveitch was visibly
disappearing before our eyes. At last, with a final gulp,
the crocodile swallowed my cultured friend entirely,
this time leaving no trace of him. From the outside of

the crocodile we could see the protuberances of Ivan Matveitch's figure as he passed down the inside of the monster. I was on the point of screaming again when destiny played another treacherous trick upon us. The crocodile made a tremendous effort, probably oppressed by the magnitude of the object he had swallowed, once more opened his terrible jaws, and with a final hiccup he suddenly let the head of Ivan Matveitch pop out for a second, with an expression of despair on his face. In that brief instant the spectacles dropped off his nose to the bottom of the tank. It seemed as though that despairing countenance had only popped out to cast one last look on the objects around it, to take its last farewell of all earthly pleasures.

No less enterprising than the crocodile's German owner, who raises the price for viewing his animal now that it contains a respectable Russian citizen, Ivan Matveitch sets about launching his new career from within the beast, delusions of grandeur inflating the situation to absurd proportions. Every utterance of his, he declares, will be listened to, thought over, repeated, printed; all will recognize what great talents have disappeared into the monster's belly. Accordingly, he instructs his wife to establish a salon, for an evening gathering of the savants, poets, philosophers, foreign statesmen, who will have conversed with him, at the zoo, in the morning:

"To be ready for anything let Elena Ivanovna buy to-morrow the Encyclopedia edited by Andrey Kraevsky, that she may be able to converse on any topic. Above all, let her be sure to read the political leader in the *Petersburg News,* comparing it every day with the *Voice.* I imagine that the proprietor will consent to take me sometimes with the crocodile to my wife's brilliant *salon.* I will be in a tank in the middle of the magnificent drawing-room, and I will scintillate with witticisms which I will prepare in the morning. To the statesmen I will impart my projects; to the poet I will speak in rhyme; with the ladies I can be amusing and charming without impropriety, since I shall be no danger to their husbands' peace of mind. . . .

"Crocodile—*crocodillo*—is evidently an Italian word, dating perhaps from the Egyptian Pharaohs, and evidently derived from the French verb *croquer,* which means to eat, to devour. . . . All these remarks I intend to deliver as my first lecture in Elena Ivanovna's *salon* when they take me there in the tank."

—Fyodor Dostoevsky, "The Crocodile"

The Crustacean'd Coiffure of Edith Sitwell

It was delightful to watch Miss Sitwell. Her face was rather llamalike, but she had a gift amounting to genius for adapting it to a "period." When she spoke of the Elizabethan it assumed a jeweled symmetry. She touched an imaginary ruffle and fingered an invisible necklace. When I mentioned the medieval she looked Gothic instantaneously. Her voice grew liturgical, her hands were peaked in prayer, even the wrinkles of her dress assumed a sculptural rigidity. . . .

The butler slid past with a tray of boiled shrimps. Edmund Wilson approached the sofa with a glass in his hand. He plucked a shrimp from the tray and dipped it in the mayonnaise.* He held it in the air as he sipped his whisky. I watched him with frozen horror as the shrimp slid from its toothpick and gracefully landed on Miss Sitwell's coiffure. But Miss Sitwell ignored it and continued with serenity.

"It is always the incantatory element which basically appeals to me. In *Paradise Lost* the incantatory is dom-

---

* mayonnaise: Robert Louis Stevenson went to meet his maker as he was making mayonnaise on the island of Samoa.

inant. 'The Ancient Mariner'† is a murmuration of the cryptomagical. And as for Eliot . . .″

" 'The Hollow Men' is pure incantation," said Edmund Wilson. He kept peering at the shrimp with a scrupulous curiosity. "I heard Eliot read it aloud once. It was a marvel of rhythmicality."

"Even in Dryden," said Miss Sitwell, "there is a sense of abracadabra. When I read Dryden I can hear the tom-toms beating in the jungle. Now with Pope it is different. There is still a hint of incantation but it has risen to a fragile, almost crystalline tinkle . . .″

I kept staring at the shrimp with a feverish fascination. It lay poised on Miss Sitwell like an amulet of ivory. I visualized it in terms of the Victorian, the Elizabethan, the Gothic. I suddenly began rather to like Edith Sitwell.

—Frederic Prokosch, *Voices*

† Ancient Mariner: For a more youthful mariner, with a brighter ordeal, see "Still Life at Sea: Manet at Sixteen"

❧ The Guest Is Gone

Dear Sister,

After you went, a low wind warbled through the house like a spacious bird, making it high but lonely. When you had gone the love came. I supposed it would. The supper of the heart is when the guest is gone.

—Emily Dickinson

❧ The Cronopio Conspiracy

A fama had a wall clock, and each week he wound it VERY VERY CAREFULLY. A cronopio passed and noting this, he began to laugh, and went home and invented an artichoke clock, or rather a wild-artichoke clock, for it can and ought to be called both ways.

This cronopio's wild-artichoke clock is a good artichoke of the larger species, fastened by its stem to a hole in the wall. Its innumerable leaves indicate what hour it is, all the hours in fact, in such a way that the cronopio has only to pluck a leaf to know what time it is. So he continues plucking them from left to right, always the leaf corresponds to that particular hour, and every day the cronopio begins pulling off a new layer of leaves. When he reaches the center, time cannot be measured, and in the infinite violet-rose of the artichoke heart the cronopio finds great contentment. Then he eats it with oil, vinegar, and salt and puts another clock in the hole.

—Julio Cortázar, "Clocks," *Cronopios and Famas*

❧ *This piece inspired a stuffed artichoke called Eaten Alive by Time at the Comida dell' Arte restaurant* in Baby Buenos Aires. An order placed, the tables were turned and all diners were ordered by the waiter to remove their watches and constraining clothing and to linger till closing time. Still alive by then, they were further ordered to leave not the way they came, and to practice absenteeism the following day at work.*

* The restaurant failed when it succeeded too close to home in its secret purpose: the Cronopiosization of the world. The waiters began playing with the customers, allowing—even inviting!—them to eat from their hands, which infected them with the artichokes' magical properties. Had the restaurant not gone under on its own account, it would have been shut down by the city fathers, anyway, as too many citizens were getting the point of these thistles and were deserting their alarm clocks for moonlight bandolinas and breakfast in bed.

Breakfast in Bed, after "Salt"
in *The Red Shoes and Other
Tattered Tales*

*Liebensraum*ing and wanderlusting all over the globe
was hardly her idea of fun, but the dominions de-
manded constant affection: there were strings attached
to the violins that had to be tautened, vibrated, and
tweaked; and then her crafty trust would go and set itself adrift in his Islands of Lingerhands while chocolate kisses melted in the newmown soon. And as for the
defrosting icebox where her lips turned blue and her
lapses, lazuli—well, the ponies were mounting the soprano and the dancer was banging on the *chapeaux*.
And just as she'd reach for a handful of one of them,
they'd go striding off into the t.v. set and leave her with
nothing but concupiscences of *café au lait* for her
petit déjeuner: wide open to his carousals,* that is.

* "*wide open to his carousals*": In the penguin's versions of these
glorious mornings (undaunted by that initial syncope during *La Bo-
hème*, he eventually became the opera critic for *Le Figaro* and a con-
sultant for Guerlain), we read "wide open to his Carusos" and the
rest of the story suddenly sidesteps into the Processional of *Aïda*,
with the soprano (so thoroughly thawed out she was now a con-
tralto—and much more to our lovers' taste) straddling the pony
where a camel is usually seen humping his way across the stage.

"Why wait till *midi* for the *plat du jour?*" they cried, "when the horses devours come at dawn?" But she kept jumping up and clattering cups and saucers and stirring the room with her hair. "Come on over here and get your back on your pedestal, or back on your pestle, anyway—or I'll mortar you and shadow your bones!"

Don't imagine such words were lost on her! She clambered directly, on the double, back into his *amour*, and then he had two of her on his hands.

—Karen Elizabeth Gordon

Of Tables and Tablecloths

Salt and the center of the world have to be there, in
that spot on the tablecloth.

—Julio Cortázar

The room had once been the dining room, and it still
contained a long table with room for eight or ten people, made of wood that was now almost black. Seinecé
used to leave dictionaries open on it, together with piles
of books, blotters of various colors, and red and yellow
pencils. He didn't leave things lying about, though: all
the articles were carefully arranged. He loved the table
with a jealous affection. He wanted to give the impression that several people lived there and all sat and
worked at the table together. He wouldn't let anyone
touch it, or even stretch out a hand toward it. That
would have amounted to handling an object imbued
with magic, like a flying carpet, and perhaps destroying
its power. Three Quinquet oil lamps converted to electricity and placed in a triangle on the table indicated
three places, as in a library reading room. When
Seinecé sat in the first place with his back to the wall,
he suddenly became a red-nosed old monk with magnifying spectacles, working at a Latin manuscript with

gray-mittened hands. Sitting facing the window he was an Assyrian deciphering a slab of clay, conjuring up the days when the language of Sumer was still spoken, when women were beautiful and manners gentle and friendly. When he sat with his back to the bed, a Chinese mandarin slowly smoothed out a little silk handkerchief, mixed the ink, and dreamed of the face of the woman he loved, tossing in bed hot-eyed and unable to sleep.

—Pascal Quignard, *The Salon in Württemberg*

. . . that tablecloth, which Augusta dreamily remembered with flying faces, had shown the delicate patience of its creation, and far from being destroyed every night like the cloth in one of the most memorable of vigils, it went on through infinite nights where bees were carding a stalactite of fabulous interwoven fibers.

—José Lezama Lima, *Paradiso*

Paradiso Parchment Pudding

José Cemí remembered the Aladdin-like days when Grandmother would get up in the morning and say, "Today I feel like making a pudding . . ." . . . Then the whole house was at the old lady's disposal. . . . She asked what boat had brought the cinnamon, then held it aloft by the root for a long time and ran the tips of her fingers over the surface, the way one tests the antiquity of a parchment, not by the date of the work hidden in it but by the width, by the boldness of the boar's tooth that engraved the surface. She lingered even more over the vanilla, not pouring it directly from the bottle, but with drops soaking her handkerchief, and afterwards, in irreversible cycles of time that only she could measure, she went on sniffing until the message from that dizzying essence faded away, and only then would she pronounce it worthy of participation in a dessert mixed by her. . . . She reestablished herself with loving domination, . . . and said to the Colonel, "Get the irons ready to singe the meringue, because soon we'll paint a mustache on Mont Blanc," voiced with an almost invisible laugh, intimating that the creation of a dessert elevated the house toward the supreme essence. "Now don't beat eggs in milk. Mix the two after you beat them separately; each should

grow in itself, and then you put together what they've
blossomed into." The sum total of these delicacies
would be put on the fire as Doña Augusta, watching it
boil, saw it form into the yellow ceramic-like pieces,
served on plates with a dark red surface, a red that
came out of night.

—José Lezama Lima, *Paradiso*

◌ Apples of Eden Electrified

A bright apple of light flared, then a second and a
third, and a line of electric apples now marked out the
Nevsky Prospect, where all night long cheap restaurants display their blood red signs, beneath which
feathered ladies dart, amidst top hats, cap-bands,
bowlers.

—Andrei Bely, *Petersburg*

Marusya Vesnitskaya's long braids would swing in time
with the waltz. They got in her way, and without stopping the dance she would hold them to her breast. She
would look up arrogantly, with half-closed eyelids, at
the delighted spectators. . . .

Little did I imagine then that the life of Marusya
Vesnitskaya was going to turn out more strangely that
the fantasies I made up. At that time one of the sons of
the King of Siam was a student in England, either at
Cambridge or Oxford. This prince could not stand
ocean travel, so he went home from England by the
long land route—across Europe, Russia and India.

During one of these trips the prince got pneumonia
on the way near Kiev. The trip was interrupted. The
prince was taken to Kiev, put up in the Tsar's palace,
and attended by the city's best doctors. The prince re-

covered, but before continuing his journey to Siam, it was necessary for him to rest and convalesce. So the prince lived in Kiev for two months. He was bored. Everyone tried to distract him—they took him to balls at the Merchants' Assembly, to the circus, and to the theater.

At one of these balls the yellow-faced prince saw Marusya Vesnitskaya. She was dancing a waltz, just as on the skating rink, her braids hanging down over her breast and her deep blue eyes looking up arrogantly under their half-opened lids. The prince was fascinated. A small man, with slanting eyes and hair that shone like wax, he danced with Marusya until drops of sweat stood out on his round face.

The prince fell in love with Marusya. He went back to Siam, but he soon returned incognito to Kiev and asked Marusya to be his bride. She agreed. . . .

Marusya went off to Siam. Soon the king died of some kind of tropical disease. Then the first two heirs to the throne died of the same disease. Marusya's husband was the king's third son. He had had very little hope of ever becoming king. But after the death of his brothers, he was the only heir, and succeeded to the throne. And the cheerful schoolgirl from Kiev, Marusya Vesnitskaya, became Queen of Siam.

The courtiers hated this foreigner as their queen. Her very existence violated all the traditions of the Siamese court. On Marusya's demand, electric lights

were installed in Bangkok, and this filled the courtiers'
cup of hatred to overflowing. They decided to poison
this queen who was upsetting all the old customs of the
people. So they began little by little to put tiny pieces
of glass from broken electric light bulbs in her food. In
six months, Marusya died of intestinal hemorrhage.

The king built a monument over her grave. An
enormous elephant of black marble, with a golden
crown on its head and its trunk hanging down sadly,
stands up to its knees in heavy grass. Underneath this
grave lies Marusya Vesnitskaya—the young Queen of
Siam.

—Konstantin Paustovsky, *The Story of a Life*

Three Poets by Lemon-Light

A crate of lemons discharges
light like a battery

> —Galway Kinnell

There would have to be bread, some rich, whole-grain bread and zwieback, and perhaps on a long, narrow dish some pale Westphalian ham laced with strips of white fat like an evening sky with bands of clouds. There would be some tea ready to be drunk, yellowish golden tea in glasses with silver saucers, giving off a faint fragrance. . . . Huge lemons, cut into slices, would sink like setting suns into the dusky sea, softly illuminating it with their radiating membranes, and its clear, smooth surface aquiver from the rising bitter essence.

> —Rainer Maria Rilke, letter to his wife

Following the Norman conquest of Sicily in the eleventh century, the Normans who remained there became besotted with the pleasures of Moslem culture. As John McPhee tells the story in Oranges:

Austere knights of Honfleur and Bayeux suddenly appeared in the streets of Palermo wearing flowing desert robes, and attracted to themselves harems of staggering diversity, while the Church raged. Normans built their own alhambras. The Normans went Muslim with such remarkable style that even Muslim poets were soon praising the new Norman Xanadus. Of one such place, which included nine brooks and a small lake with an island covered with lemon and orange trees, the poet Abd ur-Rahman Ibn Mohammed Ibn Omar wrote:

> *The oranges of the Island are like blazing fire*
> *Amongst the emerald boughs*
> *And the lemons are like the paleness of a lover*
> *Who has spent the night crying . . .*

The Subtle Flavors of a Paris Omnibus

This particular bus had a certain taste. Curious, but undeniable. All buses don't have the same taste. That's often said, but it's true. Just try the experiment. This one—an S, not to make too great a mystery of it—had the suspicion of a flavour of grilled peanuts, not to go into too great detail. The platform had its own special bouquet, peanuts not just grilled but trodden as well. One metre 60 above the trampolin, a gourmand, only there wasn't one there, would have been able to taste something rather sourish which was the neck of a man of about thirty. And twenty centimetres higher still, the refined palate was offered the rare opportunity of sampling a plaited cord just slightly tinged with the flavour of cocoa. Next we sampled the chewing gum of dispute, the chestnuts of irritation, the grapes of wrath and a bunch of bitterness.

Two hours later we were entitled to the dessert: an overcoat button . . . a real delicacy.

—Raymond Queneau, *Exercises in Style*

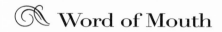 Word of Mouth

Is the unspeakable slowly growing in your mouth?
—Rainer Maria Rilke, *Sonnets to Orpheus*

The oral "chewing" of the words had a dual purpose.
The act of prayer was closely associated with reading
aloud. The words written in a prayer would therefore
take on added significance through being spoken. The
reading of holy text was more a matter of savouring di-
vine wisdom than of seeking information. Reading was
almost an act of meditation. It was said of Peter the
Venerable of Cluny that "without resting, his mouth
ruminated the sacred words." And in the 1090s St
Anselm wrote about the act of reading: "taste the
goodness of your Redeemer . . . chew the honeycomb
of his words, suck their flavour which is sweeter than
honey, swallow their wholesome sweetness; chew by
thinking, suck by understanding, swallow by loving
and rejoicing."
—James Burke, *The Day the Universe Changed*

Human speech is like a cracked kettle on which we beat
out tunes for bears to dance to, while all the time we
long to touch the stars to tears.
—Gustave Flaubert, *Madame Bovary*

Soda Shop of the Soul

Ah, Ye Gods of Gluttony! That first taste, the mouthful of froth, the sweet of the chocolate, the brisk tang of the soda, the ecstasy of the now-you-have-it, now-you-haven't, which sends you on for fulfillment into the first bite of ice cream irrigated with the lovely fluid of the soda.

Rich though these rewards be, they are nothing to the grand finale, the climax of enjoyment, when with froth gone, ice cream gone, you discard the straws, lift the glass, tilt back your head and subject your tonsils to the first superb shock of the pure Ichor of the soda, syrup, bubble water, water, melted ice cream, all blended into one Ambrosia of flavor, action, and chill.

—S. J. Perelman, "Genuflection in the Sun"

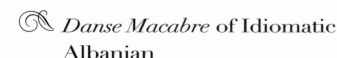 *Danse Macabre* of Idiomatic Albanian

Something strange was happening to me lately. Everyday words or expressions, things I had heard dozens of times, were suddenly taking on new meanings in my mind. The words were casting off their usual idiomatic sense. Expressions made up of two or three words would agonizingly decompose. If I heard someone say "My head is boiling," despite myself I couldn't help imagining a head boiling like a pot of beans. Words had a certain force in their normal frozen state. But now, as they began to melt and break apart, they released a stunning energy. Their decomposition scared me. I did all I could to stop it, but in vain. Chaos reigned in my head as words, devoid of logic and reality, abandoned themselves to their *danse macabre*. Everyday curses like "May you devour your head" tormented me most of all. The horrific vision of someone holding his head in his hands and devouring it was compounded by the trouble I had understanding how anyone could eat his own head when everyone knows you eat with your teeth and teeth are in the head, cursed or otherwise.

—Ismail Kadare, *Chronicle in Stone*

All this takes place in a city so steep that Kadare says:

"if you slipped and fell in the street, you might well land on the roof of a house—a peculiarity known most intimately to drunks. . . . In some places you could walk down the street, stretch out your arm, and hang your hat on a minaret."

 Suicide Hors d'Oeuvres

In Michel Tournier's "Death and the Maiden," the maiden Melanie, whose early fascination with the torments of saints develops into a romance with deadly mushrooms, a rope and a chair, a pistol in a holster, and a made-to-order guillotine, is fighting boredom from the very first paragraph, where we meet her eating lemons in the back of the classroom. Is it through food that this precocious suicide expresses her rebellion against the grayness of life around her before passing beyond symbols and metaphor, and turning to more serious measures.

Quite early in life she had identified those elements of an alimentary order that tended to precipitate her fits of boredom and those which, on the other hand, had the power of warding them off. Cream, butter, and jam—the childish food that people were always trying to press on her—foreshadowed and provoked the advancing tide of grayness, the engulfment of life in a dense, viscid slime. On the other hand, pepper, vinegar, and unripe apples—everything acid, sour, or highly spiced—exuded a breath of fresh, sparkling, invigorating air into the stagnating atmosphere. It was the difference between lemonade and milk. For Melanie, these two drinks symbolized good and evil. In spite of the protests of her family, she had adopted, as her morning drink, tea made with mineral water and flavored with a slice of lemon. And with it a very hard biscuit or a piece of nearly burned toast. On the other hand, she had been forced to give up the afternoon slice of bread and mustard she coveted because it gave rise to gales of laughter in the school playground. She had realized that with her bread and mustard she was going beyond the bounds of what was tolerated in a provincial primary school.

ℛ First Loves

I grew up kissing books and bread.

In our house, whenever anyone dropped a book or let fall a chapati or a "slice," which was our word for a triangle of buttered leavened bread, the fallen object was required not only to be picked up but also kissed, by way of apology for the act of clumsy disrespect. I was as careless and butterfingered as any child and, accordingly, during my childhood years, I kissed a large number of "slices" and also my fair share of books.

Devout households in India often contained, and still contain, persons in the habit of kissing holy books. But we kissed everything. We kissed dictionaries and atlases. We kissed Enid Blyton novels and Superman comics. If I'd ever dropped the telephone directory I'd probably have kissed that, too.

All this happened before I had ever kissed a girl. In fact it would almost be true, true enough for a fiction writer, anyhow, to say that once I started kissing girls, my activities with regard to bread and books lost some of their special excitement. But one never forgets one's first loves.

—Salman Rushdie, "Is Nothing Sacred?"
in *Imaginary Homelands*

A Crust of Terror,
a Narcotic Ritual

So Mme. Cloche sat down on a bank, quite determined
to turn back. But the path behind her wound its way
through the fields so ruthlessly, so drearily, that it terri-
fied her. She imagined what might happen to her: a
tramp might rape her, a highwayman might kill her, a
dog might bite her, a bull might charge her; two tramps
might rape her, three highwaymen might kill her, four
dogs might bite her, five bulls might charge her; seven
tramps might bite her, eight highwaymen might
charge her, nine dogs might kill her, ten bulls might
rape her. A great big caterpillar might fall down her
neck; a bat might go ooh! ooh! in her ear; a night
bird might pierce her eyes and dig them out of their
sockets. A corpse in the middle of the path; a ghost
taking her by the hand; a skeleton eating a piece of
bread.

—Raymond Queneau, *The Bark Tree*

Bread—a polyvalent object on which life, death and
dreams depend—becomes a cultural object in impoverished societies, the culminating point and instrument,
real and symbolic, of existence itself: a dense, poly-

valent paste of manifold virtue in which the nutritive function intermingles with the therapeutic (herbs, seeds and curative pastes were mixed into the bread), magico-ritual suggestion with the ludico-fantastical, narcotic and hypnotic.

—Piero Camporesi

In Bread of Dreams, *Piero Camporesi shows how through centuries of European history, most of the population was in a drugged or hallucinogenic state from starvation or the many unpredictable ingredients that wound up in the bread, which could contain anything, dead or alive. And, as a matter of fact, a skeleton eating a piece of bread would have been a common sight.*

"To whom goes this bowl?" the host cried out, picking up the first plate, obviously knowing the words of this little performance by heart.

"To me the honors, to you the treat!" Vassilia replied, covering her eyes with her hair in order to make an impartial decision. "To the young master, that his bread may not pass the night at another's doorstep!"

—Milorad Pavić, *Landscape Painted with Tea*

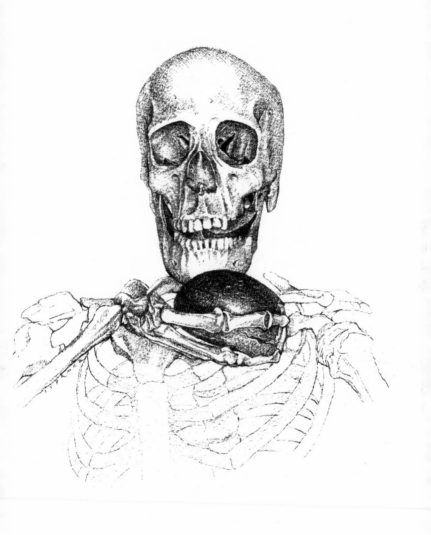

A Fate Worse than Cheesecake

The sun was very warm and there was the sound of music gradually coming nearer. A boat passed with a gramophone with a large green horn. A man in a striped blazer was punting, and a woman with golden hair sat under a red parasol. She changed a record on the gramophone and a grunting, wailing organ filled the air. "How I hate organs" thought Emma, "I'm sure people who like organs eat cheese cakes and call their drawing rooms lounges." She lay on her back imagining the golden haired woman sitting in her lounge, eating eternal cheese cakes and listening to a fruity organ. She would have several little girls she called "the kiddies." They would have crimped hair with large pink bows on the top, and wear patent-leather shoes and shiny satin bridesmaids' frocks on summer Sundays.

—Barbara Comyns

The central drama of this book, Who Was Changed and Who Was Dead, *is unleashed by a very well-meaning baker who decides to surprise the village and surrounding countryside with a wild new bread. It is, much to his sur-*

prise, a fatal* experiment, for the bread is rye, and rye tainted with the mold of ergot that produces hallucinations, hysterics, and death.

⟨⟩ Two Weddings

⟨⟩ *In Gustave Flaubert's* Madame Bovary, *Charles and Emma are married in grandly farmhouse style, with a tawdry tiered wedding cake painstakingly fashioned by a pastry cook new to the district:*

It started off at the base with a square of blue cardboard; this square held a temple with porticoes and colonnades and stucco statuettes in niches studded with gilt-paper stars; there came next on the second layer a castle in meringue surrounded by minute fortifications in candied angelica, almonds, raisins, and quarters of orange and finally, on the uppermost platform, which represented a green meadow with rocks, lakes of jam, and nutshell boats, a little cupid sat in a chocolate swing whose two uprights had two real rosebuds for knobs at the top.

---

* Not for our heroine, Emma, whose fantasy of children and cheesecakes shows the spirit of a true survivor.

Such a folly (and as a matter of fact, devotees of archi-tectural follies on a spree from England in France con-sumed a cake that was made according to Flaubert's description, down to the last detail) is just asking for trouble, from another extreme: a pugnacious Paris bistro called the Molehill, as described by the Captain to his audience sharing drinks in another establishment:

"It was just striking three. The *Taupinière* had barely opened and already you could hardly get in, just like every night, there were butchers, citizens, drivers, car-men, swankers, lushes and quite a bit of young stuff and ass. . . . I finished one glass, another, a third, a fourth, laughing to myself, biding my time, looking at the mugs on all of them and enjoying myself hugely for there's always a hell of a shindy at the *Taupinière* and the kind of arguments and wisecracking and scrap-ping I like goes on there all the time. I was on the look-out for squalls, for you never know how far things will go. Words flying through the air, addressed to nobody special, they can carry a long way and do a lot of dam-age, more than a bazooka can do to a Panzer. I drank away, having a laugh all to myself, and what do I see but that fat Charlotte at the cash, who's been putting the eye on me for some while, like a frog, and if she doesn't make a sign to her husband and go jibbering I don't know what in his ear, and there's that great slob of a Jules, I never could stand his guts, turning his head to stare me down in his turn, and what does he do but start over towards me with a big smile and his glass in his hand to drink my health and get better acquainted; well, thinks I, this is it, and I let him have one to the head and empty my glass in his face, that old bastard who used to boot me out when I was a kid and wouldn't even let me park myself by the stove on rainy nights. Pow! Have that, you old swine, and all of a sudden it's a brawl, you'd think the crowd was waiting for nothing else but that, to start jumping on each other and bashing each other about fit to wreck the joint. Soda siphons were flying, glasses, bottles. The little tables were crushed, the desserts, the piles of plates, the platters of *hors d'oeuvres*, the dishes of radishes. One type was soaking starched serviettes in the sauces and mayonnaise and hurling handfuls of them into the mêlée. Talk about a brawl! What with the butchers who'd taken the bar by storm under pretext of helping the owner, but were really looting it and stripping it, beating each other over the head like Punch and Judy with salamis they'd unhooked from the ceiling at the back, you'd have thought it was a massacred wedding party what with their bonnets and their white aprons all smeared with the blood of the abattoirs."

—Blaise Cendrars, *To the End of the World*

ℛ Heart in a Soup Spoon

She decided that this friendship had laid the founda-
tion for my career, and she baked a jam struedel and a
poppy-seed cake for the guest. The heart of our race,
the heart that faces struggle with such endurance, was
in these pastries.

—Isaac Babel

He was very curious: he wanted to see everything in
Berlin; but for him, "everything" meant the *people,*
and indeed all kinds of people, not those who hung out
in the artists' restaurants and the fancy pubs. His favorite place was Aschinger's restaurant. There we stood
side by side, very slowly eating a pea soup.* With his
globular eyes behind his very thick eyeglasses, he
looked at the people around us, every single one, all of
them, and he could never get his fill of them. He was
annoyed when he finished the soup. He wished for an
inexhaustible bowl, for all he wanted to do was keep on

* Was Thérèse Eglantine skulking nearby, or in their very bowls and
spoons? In Cendrars' *To the End of the World*, "She advanced into
the pea soup, her legs trembling, chilled to the bones." Berlin may
well have been on the way to the end of the world at the time.

looking, and since the people changed rapidly, there
was a great deal to see.

—Elias Canetti on Isaac Babel, *The Torch in My Ear*

Booed Writers à la Carte

It is splendid to be a great writer, to put men
into the frying pan of your imagination and
make them pop like chestnuts.

—Gustave Flaubert

*Friendships thriving among his French contemporaries
and Turgenev, whom Flaubert called his "bon Moscove,"
the group decided to dine together once a month, holding
what they called the "Flaubert dinner" or the "booed
writers' dinner," as each diner claimed to have had a play
of his booed in the theater. The dinners took place at
Adolphe and Pelé's behind the Opéra, over bouillabaisse
at a tavern near the Opéra Comique, or sometimes at
Voisin's.*

They all called themselves gastronomes, but their tastes differed. Flaubert thrilled to the flavors of Rouen duckling cooked *à l'estouffade*, Edmond de Goncourt thought it the last word in elegance to chew on candied ginger, Zola doted on sea urchins and shellfish, while Turgenev spooned down his caviar. "Nothing could be more delicious than dinners among friends at which people can speak openly, their wits alert and their elbows on the table," wrote Alphonse Daudet. "We would sit down to the table at seven, and at two in the morning we were still at it. Flaubert and Zola dined in their shirtsleeves, Turgenev reclined on a divan, we sent the waiters away . . . and we talked literature. . . . There was always a book by one or the other of us that had just come out. . . . We talked absolutely frankly, without flattery and without the complicity of mutual admiration."

—Henri Troyat, *Turgenev*

Pistachios: The Expletive

What say you, good masters, to a squab pigeon pasty,
some collops of venison, a saddle of veal, widgeon with
crisp hog's bacon, a boar's head with pistachios, a
bason of jolly custard, a medlar tansy and a flagon of
old Rhenish? *

    Gadzooks! cried the last speaker. That likes me well.
Pistachios!

—James Joyce, *Ulysses*

*Nino Franck recalled that while James Joyce was work-
ing on* Finnegans Wake, *he took a break to take a taxi and
take a walk (Finnegans Walk) in the Bois de Boulogne.
Having spent all afternoon making jokes out of words,
when he spoke to the chauffeur he called him "chou-
fleur"—cauliflower—leaving the man both astonished
and insulted. Joyce paid and went off laughing, telling*

---

* If Joyce had been present, that flagon of old Rhenish would have
to be cleared the minute it was drained. He'd always protest the
presence of an empty bottle on the table. As Bertie Rodgers put it
while conducting these radioed recollections of him: "Well, an
empty bottle can never go the rounds. And the round, the circle, the
recurring and reassuring routine, was all-important to Joyce,
whether in Trieste, or Zürich, or Paris."

Franck later, "You know, I looked in and really he had the head of a cauliflower."

◈ On the Floor of the *Butica*

◈ *Elias Canetti, who later in his life will observe Isaac Babel's great appetite for pea soup at Aschinger's restaurant, Berlin, as a child takes pleasure in his grandfather's wholesale grocery store, the* butica, *in Ruschuk:*

Huge, open sacks stood on the floor, containing various kinds of cereals, there was millet, barley, and rice. If my hands were clean, I was allowed to reach into the sacks and touch the grains. That was a pleasant sensation, I filled my hand, lifted it up, smelled the grains, and let them slowly run back down again; I did this often, and though there were many other strange things in the store, I liked doing that best, and it was hard to get me away from the sacks. There was tea and coffee and especially chocolate. There were huge quantities of everything, and it was always beautifully packed, it wasn't sold in small amounts as in ordinary shops. I also especially liked the open sacks on the floor because they weren't too high for me and because when I

reached in, I could feel the many grains, which meant
so much to me.

> —Elias Canetti, *The Tongue Set Free:*
> *Remembrance of a European Childhood*

The Wisdom of Chick Peas, the Wait of the Butcher

For a man like him, holed up in written reality, those
stormy sessions that began in the bookstore and ended
at dawn in the brothels were a revelation. It had never
occurred to him until then to think that literature was
the best plaything that had ever been invented to make
fun of people, as Alvaro demonstrated during one
night of revels. Some time would have to pass before
Aureliano realized that such arbitrary attitudes had
their origins in the example of the wise Catalonian, for
whom wisdom was worth nothing if it could not be
used to invent a new way of preparing chick peas.

> —Gabriel García Márquez,
> *One Hundred Years of Solitude*

It was in January 1965, while driving from Mexico City to Acapulco, that he envisioned the first chapter of the book that was to become *Cien Años*. . . . He then went home and told Mercedes: Don't bother me, especially don't bother me about money. And he went to work at the desk he called the Cave of the Mafia, in a house at number 6 Calle de La Loma, Mexico City, and working eight to ten hours a day for eighteen months, he wrote the novel.

"I didn't know what my wife was doing," he said, "and I didn't ask any questions. But there was always whiskey in the house. Good Scotch. . . . But when I was finished writing, my wife said, 'Did you really finish it? We owe twelve thousand dollars.' She had borrowed from friends for a year and a half."

At one point, he said, his wife was given the opportunity by the butcher shop, where she was a good client, to pay by the month. She refused, but later, when getting money every day was more difficult, she accepted the offer and paid monthly installments to the butcher. . . .

"She is stupendous," García said.

—William Kennedy, visiting Gabriel García Márquez in Barcelona, "The Yellow Trolley Car in Barcelona and Other Visions"

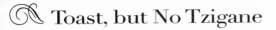 Toast, but No Tzigane

Poached eyes on ghost.

—James Joyce

Is that ghost a voyeur? Watching Ford Maddox Ford with Rebecca West? His embraces made her feel like the toast beneath a poached egg, she said.

Did you know that George Bernard Shaw was not only "a smiling sewing-machine," as Yeats said of him, but also a music critic? And that somewhere you can find his housekeeper's cookbook full of Shaw's vegetarian recipes? Here's one in this review of a performance of Mozart's overture to The Marriage of Figaro.

The concert began with Mozart's *Figaro Overture.* If you want to ascertain whether a musician is hopelessly belated, benighted, out of date, and behind his time, ask him how this overture should be played. If he replies "In three and a half minutes," away with him at once; he is guilty. . . . However, the overture, so treated, is undeniably useful to boil eggs by, though I prefer them boiled four minutes myself.

A Momentous Meeting

Joyce met Proust once at a literary dinner, and Proust
asked Joyce did he like truffles, and Joyce said yes, he
did, and I know Joyce was very amused afterwards. He
said, "Here the two greatest literary figures of our time
meet, and they ask each other if they like truffles."

—Arthur Power in W. R. Rodgers'
Irish Literary Portraits

Truffles and Toulouse-Lautrec

Paris, October 1891

My dear Mama,

I begin by reassuring you about Papa's condition, he has had a touch of influenza and treated
it at the Turkish bath. The steam room suffocated
him and after a brief fainting spell he was
quickly up on his feet thanks to a few glasses of
kümmel. . . .

I thank you for the prospective truffles. If you
send me a fowl stuffed with truffles, write on the
address the weight: Fowl so much

Truffles so much

because the excise charges are exorbitant when this precaution isn't taken.

Another thing. Towards the end of next week and towards the end of the one after have a fowl—capon or chicken—sent to me. Bourges' brother, who usually supplies the poultry, is off on a two-week trip.

Has the goose-liver season started? If it has, remember to have a dozen tins sent to me. I am re-reading my letter and find it to have a gastronomic character. My poster is pasted today on the walls of Paris and I'm going to do another one. . . .

I kiss you,

Yours,
Henri

—Henri de Toulouse-Lautrec

Samizdat Shopping List

* In his journal/novel* The Dream Diary,* *which chronicles his moods, movements through pre–Velvet Revolution Prague, flirtations, harassments endured,† the departures/exile of numerous friends, the seasonal cycle in his garden at Dobrichovice, the literary projects that he publishes and distributes in manuscript form,‡ Ludvík Vaculík reports an exchange with his wife, Madla, as he leaves Dobrichovice alone for Prague—her parting orders to him:*

Take currants to her aunt, stay at home, write, and, depending on what's available, buy, cook, and bring a little chicken. *Ludvík:* "My God, why do you say a little chicken?" "Because it doesn't have to be big." "No! You're lying! You say so to make me think it's less work!" *Laughing, she admits he's right.*

---

* The kitchen is the setting for much of this book: it's where there's warmth, where Vaculík works.
† And drunk repeatedly in *A Cup of Coffee with My Interrogator.*
‡ Typewritten, carbon copies through Vaculík's *Padlock Editions.*

◌ Cakes and Jam for the Marquis de Sade

◌ From the Bastille in the 1780s the Marquis de Sade wrote letters to his wife that are, writes John Russell in Paris, *"among the most magnificent in the history of invective." In truth, these letters show the relative liberty and comfort of the well-born and wealthiest prisoners. In September 1784, he wrote:*

"Air and fruit are the two things I live by and, especially in this season, I would as soon have my throat cut as forgo them. If you saw the abominable, debased, and stinking vittles that are served to us here, you would understand that anyone who is used to a more delicate diet must needs supplement it with purchases of his own . . . so please take note of this list

A basket of fruit, made up of

Peaches	12
Nectarines	12
Poires de beurre	12
Bunches of grapes	12

(half of these to be ripe, and the rest ready to eat in 3 or 4 days)

Two pots of jam

A dozen cakes from the Palais Royal (six of them
orange-flavored) and two pounds of sugar.
Three packets of candles for the night.

*I have chatted with several other illustrious guests of the
Bastille,* and have come back from these discussions
with the following typical menu which one prisoner cited
(in a pamphlet he circulated after his release) to demon-
strate the rigors and deprivations within:*

Green pea soup, garnished with lettuce and a
joint of fowl

Sliced roast beef, garnished with parsley

Meat pie, garnished with sweetbreads, coxcombs,
asparagus, mushrooms, and truffles

Sheep's tongue *en ragoût*

Biscuit, Fruit, Burgundy wine

* Including Richelieu, Voltaire, the Cardinal de Rohan, the Marquis
de Mirabeau, and the Abbé de Moncrif, debtor, debaucher of girls,
and fomenter of rebellion in an ecclesiastic jail, where he also flus-
tered his superiors by raising chickens and ducks in his rooms.

ℛ La Cucina Futurista

ℛ The Futurist Cookbook, *from Marinetti and his pals, prefigures Fascist ideals, kicks pasta out of La Cucina Italiana (with a chorus of pasta-bashing supporters that includes Schopenhauer), and offers the following recipe by Aeropainter Fillia for "A Simultaneous Dinner," which would go quite convivially with laptop computers and cellular phones. The latter could easily be adapted to dispensing campari and spumoni as well as dismusica and words:*

For businessmen unable in the whirl of affairs to get to a restaurant or return home a simultaneous meal will be designed which will allow them to continue various activities (writing, walking, talking) and eat contemporaneously:

A big smoker's pipe of lacquered red metal with a little electric oven will cook a soup.

Some small "thermos" bottles in the form of fountain pens, filled with hot chocolate.

Some pocket diaries will contain fish pastilles.

Letters and invoices of different strengths of perfume will be available in a file to calm, satisfy or excite the appetite.

Abduction in a Bowl of Borscht

With what gusto I ate! How delicious it was. It was
Greek, southern fare. Powerfully, like the body of a
bull, a whole green pepper lay in the borsch, displaying
its side like the bull that abducted Europa.

—Yury Olesha, *No Day without a Line*

Olives and Orvieto
in Alexandria

It was cold in the street and I crossed to the lighted
blaze of shops in Rue Fuad. In a grocer's window I saw
a small tin of olives with the name *Orvieto* on it, and
overcome by a sudden longing to be on the right side
of the Mediterranean, entered the shop; bought it; had
it opened there and then; and sitting down at a marble
table in that gruesome light I began to eat Italy, its dark
scorched flesh, hand-modelled spring soil, dedicated
vines.

—Lawrence Durrell, *Justine*

◈ The Gaze of a Dandy Piecrust

Some gaze as if from a fog; others are even worse—as if embedded in dough. Just like such a pie-crust decoration, Anatole Marienhof looked at me in a restaurant yesterday. Good Lord, the handsome dandy Marienhof!
—Yury Olesha, *No Day without a Line*

◈ *Gogol, too, has a way with piecrusts, used in his story "Ivan Fyodorovich Shponka and His Aunt" to show how the aunt can think of nothing but getting Ivan Fyodorovich married off immediately so she can bustle about and fuss over her great-nephews:*

Often, when making a pie, . . . she forgot herself and, fancying that a little child was standing beside her and asking for a bit of the pie, she would absent-mindedly hold out her hand with the best bit to him, and the watchdog, taking advantage of this heaven-sent opportunity, seized the tasty morsel and brought her out of her reverie by his loud champing. . . . She even gave up her favourite occupations and did not go hunting, especially after she had shot a crow instead of a partridge, a thing that had never happened to her before.

Sleeping It Off in Baden-Baden Far from the Konditorei

March 1987

Dear Silvia,

As the surgeon had assured me, the operation went off as neatly, down to every detail, as The Appenzeller Heist. This is the first day I've felt alive since succumbing completely to the anesthesia. For three days I did nothing but sleep, for dreaming seemed the most exciting thing around to do. Giant typewriters stored in a sort of lawnmower shed, me dancing with a Chilean architect on a wet floor in his underwear, and this morning Princess Diana giving birth to six babies beside an Alice-in-Wonderland garden/grotto whose every object was edible, even the lawn chairs, and I was breaking off pieces of everything and tasting them—all bonbons, my dear.

Laku noć
Yolanta

Bonbons over Petersburg

This is from Chapter the Fifth of Petersburg, *in which an account is given of the little fellow with the wart by his nose and of the sardine tin with horrible contents. The time is 1905, the city is Petersburg. Young Nikolai has been seduced by a band of terrorists into bombing his own father, a high government official. I don't want to give away the story, but I can tell you that Petersburg is more than merely a backdrop: the city itself is a character, and an immortal one, thanks to Bely's blazing and inno-vative work.*

"A bonbonniere . . .

"Wha-a-a . . . ?

"A ribbon!"

And when he had torn the ribbon loose, his hopes were shattered (he had been hoping for something). Be-neath the pink ribbon, the bonbonniere contained—not sweet candies from Ballet's, but a small tin.

Then, he happened to notice a clock mechanism at-tached to the side. There was a little metal key which had to be turned so that the small sharp black hand would point to the hour. . . . The little key slowly turned to one o'clock, then to two o'clock, and Nikolai

Apollonovich jumped off to the side. He glanced at the desk out of the corner of his eye. There lay a small tin containing oily sardines (on one occasion he had made himself sick on sardines, and ever since then he had not touched them). A sardine tin, an ordinary sardine tin: with rounded corners. . . .

"No!"

A sardine tin with horrible contents!

And a life incomprehensible to the mind had already erupted, and the hour hand, the minute hand now crawled, and the nervous fine hair that indicated the seconds began skipping around the circle—until the instant when—

> —the horrible contents of the sardine tin would expand in a rush, uncontrollably; then: the sardine tin would fly apart. . . .
> —the gases would briskly spread in circles, tearing the desk to bits with a thunderous roar, and something would burst with a boom inside him; and his body would be blown to bits; mixed with the splinters, mixed with the gases, it would splatter in slush;
> —in a hundredth of a second the walls would collapse, and the contents, expanding, would whirl off into the wan sky in splinters, stones, and blood.

Shaggy dense smoke would billow and unfurl and tail onto the Neva. . . .

His ears twitched. He felt nauseated, as if he had swallowed the bomb like a pill. There was a bloating sensation in the pit of his stomach.

He would never crush it, never!

The only thing left was to throw it into the Neva, but there was still time for that. He had only to turn the little key twenty times more and everything would be postponed. But he dawdled, and sank into an armchair with no strength left. He was overcome by drowsiness. His power of thought was weakened, and as it broke away from his body, it sketched meaningless, idle arabesques of some kind. . . .

—Andrei Bely, *Petersburg*

Nabokov, who put Petersburg *right up there with Joyce's* Ulysses *and Proust's* In Search of Lost Time *as the greatest works of twentieth-century fiction, was asked in an interview with Robert Hughes what scenes he would like to have filmed. His answer includes one scene that stars a sardine (this one isn't loaded):*

Herman Melville at breakfast, feeding a sardine to his cat.

Poe's wedding, Lewis Carroll's picnics.

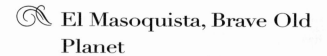 El Masoquista, Brave Old Planet

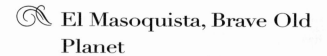 *Silvia Monrós-Stojaković and I, willed to each other by our friends Carol Dunlop and Julio Cortázar (whose novel* Hopscotch *Silvia translated into Serbo-Croatian), have known each other since 1981 through letters, books, and also friends who see us separately in New York, Paris, Croatia, and Serbia. Silvia, an Argentine, has lived in Beograd for many years. This excerpt of a letter written upon her return from Spain recounts her adventures there with Stipe Mesić, the Croatian military commander, and her very personal experience as a Serb in a war where she doesn't belong—and who does?*

Draga Kerin,

One of the best things about traveling is that
you may tell the whole story just saying hallo with a
simple post card. Another good thing is the big letter that's already waiting for you when you get back
home. . . .

In Spain I had to translate the pyrotechnical
speech Stipe Mesić made when it came his turn to
expose his views on the war that the Spanish orga-
nizers of the seminar wanted to be explained by
the representatives of all the former Yugoslavia's
courtyards. Believing that the only way I could do
my job was to do it the best one, for I believe that
that might be the way to remain what we all should
be, a good person, or at least to behave in a better
way than the side which you disagree with, I even
put some additional conviction coming from my
noblesse oblige instinct of hara-kiri, specially when
he called for bombing the naughty Serbs in
Belgrade. Besides, I consider it would be quite
tasteless even to try to prove the contrary, the official truth having as usual nothing to do with facts
and even less with ethics, not to say aesthetics.
Thus, I won't spread my theories on human history
even over you. As the Buddhists say, who knows,
doesn't speak, who speaks doesn't know. Or as you
would say, *Catch 22*.

In any case, from the professional point of view I could be proud with my own performance. Instead, I was sad.

And then came the last day, and the rector of the Menéndez y Pelayo International University invited for lunch into a knights' dining-room the participants of our seminar, together with the participants of other seminars, like the one about fluvial melioration in the Highlands or Caravaggio's painting and his time.

Once again, I was placed next to Mesić. Since I have some experience in consecutive translation during meals, I rather eat before or after, not during. During, that means that Peter can smoothly proceed to the hors d'oeuvres while Paul gives the toast, after what Paul starts to recuperate the missed lobster jumping into the hot Charlotte while Peter exclaims, O, I see, so now it's raining in your country, well, you know, we make excellent umbrellas. After that Paul clarifies that he doesn't need umbrellas, but another glass of wine, while Peter, now with undissemblied anxiety asks the waiter is there another piece of cake. During that concise menu the breathless interpreter couldn't even swallow some air having to do the talking all the time, poor Mary. So I didn't eat either at that lunch.

Mesić asked me about this, and now my friends say he asked you because he thought that food could be poisoned, but I think that at that moment this was not his way of thinking, so he just asked, and I just answered that I prefer not to eat while working, and having the impression he seemed interested, I added, Yes, now I'm working, the same as you, and we're sitting together, we sit together while doing our best, and the rector does also the same enjoying his local soup made of shells and beans, and he'd like you to enjoy it too, but you are not sure should the shells be treated with spoons, forks, or fingers, while I'm not sure shall I find my kitchen when you bomb Belgrade. Because, you see, my house is near the Army Headquarters. But I couldn't care less about the kitchen, I said. I wouldn't be sorry about it; on the contrary, I said. I said I'm not even sorry for myself.

I was sorry thinking of all the many Silvias round here that are being evaluated even more dangerous and noxious than Hussein and Khadaffi altogether by some other Silvias round the world that share Hemingway's bells, as I do, and as I always did and acted having justice in mind, as I had in 1968, for instance, thus trying to help the underdogs and thus, condemning those you've been told are guilty for breaking the harmony of this brave old planet. So I was sorry, not worried, not even about an eventual death. Dying is not such a big deal. The real pain in the ass is a mistaken life and to pass away under lies and misunderstandings after having already been punished by your own Milosescu headache.

Anyway, after that memorable lunch I was told that Mesić said he felt ashamed when Mrs. Silvia mentioned the bombs to be thrown over her kitchen. The same evening, before leaving Santander the next morning, Mesić kissed me good-bye. Well, well, said my Spanish colleague, that's something to tell the grandchildren. . . . Her husband is a very nice fellow, a young Croat she met in Zagreb while she was studying Slavistics. She's translated Pavić's novel *Landscape Painted with Tea* into Spanish. Her name is Luisa Garrido.

After Santander I did Barcelona, Seville, Granada, Madrid, Toledo and El Escorial. In Toledo what impressed me almost like El Greco's house was a poster showing a teapot having at the same side the part for pouring the tea and the part for holding the pot. The poster was for an exhibition called *Impossible Objects*, to take place in another café whose name was El Masoquista.

And then I finally made my spectacular comeback home, and ever since I've been cooking. In my kitchen. But the best thing about getting back home is that the letter that's already waiting for you starts saying "Hey there, bad guy!"

This time I'm sending you some material presented in the Santander seminar . . . and I'm also sending lots of love.

Silvia

⟋⟍ A Café in Mostar

The huge café of our hotel covered the whole ground floor, and had two billiard-tables in the centre. For dinner we ate the trout of the place . . . also a superb cheese soufflé. The meal was served with incredible delay, and between the courses we read the newspapers and looked about us. Moslems came in from the streets, exotic in fezes. They hung them up and went to their seats and played draughts and drank black coffee. Young officers moved rhythmically through the beams of white light that poured down upon the acid green of the billiard-tables, and the billiard balls gave out their sound of stoical shock. There was immanent the Balkan feeling of a shiftless yet just doom. It seemed possible that someone might come into the room, perhaps a man who would hang up his fez, and explain, in terms just comprehensible enough to make it certain they were not nonsensical, that all the people at the tables must stay there until the two officers who were playing billiards at that moment had played a million games, and that by the result their eternal fates would be decided; and that this would be accepted, and people would sit there quietly waiting and reading the newspapers.

> —Rebecca West, *Black Lamb and Grey Falcon: A Journey through Yugoslavia*

ᘒ Truth on a Plate

Vida had started early on to translate from her first mother tongue, Serbian, into German, and her house was always full of people. Serving her guests meat on Szolnay plates, Vida liked to say:

"To each person comes, like his portion of meat, his own part of the truth. But the truth, too, needs to be salted; otherwise it's tasteless. I only translate writers who can do that." . . .

Friends came to drink plum brandy on her piano and eat goat cheese with garlic from her homeland; when they sneezed the expressions on their faces would have made one think that they had at least two international reasons for doing so; and they departed content, and they came back again.

—Milorad Pavić, *Landscape Painted with Tea*

℞ Shuffled Gooseflesh

Someone shuffles by my door muttering: "Our goose is cooked."

Strange! I have my knife and fork ready. I even have the napkin tied around my neck, but the plate before me is still empty.

Nevertheless, someone continues to mutter outside my door regarding a certain hypothetical, allegedly cooked goose that he claims is ours in common.

—Charles Simic, *The World Doesn't End*

℞ *Alfred Hitchcock had declared his profession* producer *when a customs officer could not contain his curiosity and further questioned him. "What do you produce?" the officer inquired. "Gooseflesh," Hitchcock replied.*

Hitchcock, whose gourmandizing produced his own flesh, too, was once a guest at a dinner party where food was hardly in profusion. While serving the coffee, his hostess said, "I do hope that you will dine here again, Mr. Hitchcock." "By all means," he rejoined. "Let's start right now."

Soaked Boot with Swan Song

Meanwhile the smell of borsht floated through the room and agreeably tickled the nostrils of the starving guests. All streamed into the dining room. A string of ladies, talkative and silent, lean and stout, filed in ahead, and the long table was dotted with every hue. I am not going to describe all the dishes on the table! I shall say nothing of the cheese cakes and sour cream, nor of the sweetbread served in the borsht, nor of the turkey stuffed with plums and raisins, nor of the dish that looked very much like a boot soaked in kvass, nor of the sauce which is the swan song of the old cook, the sauce which is served in flaming spirit to the great diversion, and at the same time, terror of the ladies. I am not going to talk about these dishes because I greatly prefer eating them to expatiating on them in conversation.

—Nikolai Gogol, "The Tale of How Ivan Ivanovich Quarreled with Ivan Nikiforovich"

# Turgenev the Host

Evenings which were not spent at the theatre or at the houses of the socially eminent where he was welcome, were frequently devoted to hilarious gatherings of the *Contemporary* litterateurs at the flat of one of the number . . . or at a restaurant. These were very different gatherings from the ascetic and intellectually serious "circles" of the thirties and forties, of Stankevich or Belinsky, for example, where the most stimulating diet consisted of tea and dry rusks, and the topic of argument such subjects as the existence of God or the philosophy of Schelling or Hegel. At the *Contemporary* gatherings the drink was champagne, and the food plentiful and often luxurious. The usual subjects of conversation were personal gossip and literary argument. A favorite amusement was the improvisation of verse epigrams, a pastime at which Turgenev excelled. . . .

Turgenev occupied a fairly spacious apartment near the Anichkov bridge, on the Fontanka. He now had two servants—Zakhar and his cook Stepan. The cook was a great artist—Turgenev had bought him for 1,000 roubles. Stepan was devoted to Turgenev and always abandoned whatever engagements as chef he had undertaken during Turgenev's absences from St.

Petersburg in order to cook for him whenever he returned to the capital.

—Leonard Schapiro,
Turgenev: His Life and Times

Honey and oil—this comparison may be well applied to
those perfectly rounded graceful sentences of his, when
he settles down to the task of writing beautifully. . . .

Their melody is all wrong; their luster looks cheap and
their philosophy is not deep enough to justify pearl-
diving. . . . and if, at its best, his prose reminds one of
rich milk, these prose poems may be compared to
fudge.

—Vladimir Nabokov on Turgenev,
Lectures on Russian Literature

Into the Woods with Elena Ivanovna Nabokov

On overcast afternoons, all alone in the drizzle, my mother, carrying a basket (stained blue on the inside by somebody's whortleberries), would set out on a long collecting tour. Toward dinnertime, she could be seen emerging from the nebulous depths of a park alley, her small figure cloaked and hooded in greenish-brown wool, on which countless droplets of moisture made a kind of mist all around her. As she came nearer from under the dripping trees and caught sight of me, her face would show an odd, cheerless expression, which might have spelled poor luck, but which I knew was the tense, jealously contained beatitude of the successful hunter. Just before reaching me, with an abrupt, drooping movement of the arm and shoulder and a "Pouf!" of magnified exhaustion, she would let her basket sag, in order to stress its weight, its fabulous fullness.

Near a white garden bench, on a round garden table of iron, she would lay out her boletes in concentric circles to count and sort them. Old ones, with spongy, dingy flesh, would be eliminated, leaving the young and the crisp. For a moment, before they were bundled away by a servant to a place she knew nothing about, to a doom that did not interest her, she would stand there admiring them, in a glow of quiet contentment. As often happened at the end of a rainy day, the sun might cast a lurid gleam just before setting, and there, on the damp round table, her mushrooms would lie, very colorful, some bearing traces of extraneous vegetation— a grass blade sticking to a viscid fawn cap, or moss still clothing the bulbous base of a dark-stippled stem. And a tiny looper caterpillar would be there, too, measuring, like a child's finger and thumb, the rim of the table, and every now and then stretching upward to grope, in vain, for the shrub from which it had been dislodged.

—Vladimir Nabokov, *Speak, Memory*

Blazing Pages of Scented Summer

In July my father went to take the waters and left me, with my mother and elder brother, a prey to the blinding white heat of the summer days. Dizzy with light, we dipped into that enormous book of holidays, its pages blazing with sunshine and scented with the sweet melting pulp of golden pears.

On those luminous mornings Adela returned from the market, like Pomona emerging from the flames of day, spilling from her basket the colorful beauty of the sun—the shiny pink cherries full of juice under their transparent skins, the mysterious black morellos that smelled so much better than they tasted; apricots in whose golden pulp lay the core of long afternoons. And next to that pure poetry of fruit, she unloaded sides of meat with their keyboard of ribs swollen with energy and strength, and seaweeds of vegetables like dead octopuses and squids—the raw material of meals with a yet undefined taste, the vegetative and terrestrial ingredients of dinner, exuding a wild and rustic smell.

—Bruno Schulz, "August,"
in *The Street of Crocodiles*

The Taste

There is a drink which only the old ever taste. Everyone knows that the day is full of rocks, some large, some small, which move. They are all invisible and no one mentions them, but everyone knows that they are rocks. No one knows how to get past them, or to enter them, or to see what is inside them. They are said to contain the treasure of Age, which no one has ever looked on—a black treasure.

At night when only the old are awake, black springs

rise in some of the rocks and begin to flow toward some of the old. The slow streams seldom choose for destinations the old who are nearest to them. The rocks in which they rise have all moved. The withered body toward which a stream starts to make its way may have passed the source years before and not have known it. How wide the world is now! How empty! How far a stream may have to flow! Meanwhile the old are dying.

As a stream passes through the dark meadows, birds that are standing there turn to look. Each time they think it is Memory once more. But it is not Memory. Each of the birds was a color, once, and this is where they go.

When at last a stream lies on the tongue it set out for, it rests. There is a moment of trembling. Tears come out and sit in the night. After a while the stream gets up and goes to its boat and loads the old person into it and they drift away together toward the valley. In the morning the body that has been visited can no longer stand, no longer speak. It swallows and swallows as though trying to remember tasting water for the first time.

—W. S. Merwin, *Houses and Travellers*

ℛ To Tell the Tooth

ℛ *The time has come to talk a bit about teeth. The Wife of Bath, Chaucer tells us, was gat-toothed, with a space between the front ones, a tip-off to her hypersexuality. At age eleven, Nabokov had an extra tooth growing in the middle of his palate, "as if he were a young shark," his biographer says; it was taken away in Berlin. I wonder if it was to go with the other languages, especially the future adopted tongue in which he would write his masterpieces. Tommaso Landolfi (whose "Gogol's Wife" I recommend after you've read "Beyond the Bliny" in this book) wrote a story called "Words in Commotion," whose narrator is brushing his teeth. What comes out when he rinses his mouth is a garrulous gang of words, all jabbering at once, complaining about the meanings assigned to their sounds, and attempting to swap them so that each sound will henceforth stand for something else—all while performing acrobatics on the brackets of the bathroom mirror. And Blaise Cendrars'* To the End of the World *opens with Thérèse Eglantine, an aging actress, in bed with a tattooed legionnaire, positions shifting so suddenly that at one point her false teeth go flying through the air.*

Dessert to this rumination will be found in "The Golden Toothpick of Omar Khayyam."

The Rat in the Library

A rat who obviously didn't know how to read nevertheless loved books. So he set up house in a library where
no one went any longer.

He would walk on the books, between them, run
along them, contemplate them with a tear in his eye
and his mouth watering. It was his home, he was happy
there; these are my books, he said.

Occasionally, he'd stop to nibble at a part of one
book or another.

—Phew! The new books stink of glue and ink, and
their pages are flimsy and damp and stick to the
palate.

Instead, he regaled himself with the most ancient
pages, the dry and yellowed ones, which were very
crunchy, for example his old edition of Diderot's *Encyclopedia*; he would always remember the article consecrated to God, which he made quite a feast of.

There's also a telephone book dating from 1916, full
of names of dead people and obsolete addresses which
he offers bites from to his buddies when they come to
visit him, and which they highly prize.

His salon is furnished in paperbacks, colored and
pliant. The bathroom is behind the *Letters* of Madame
de Sévigné. An incunable bound in vellum whose cover

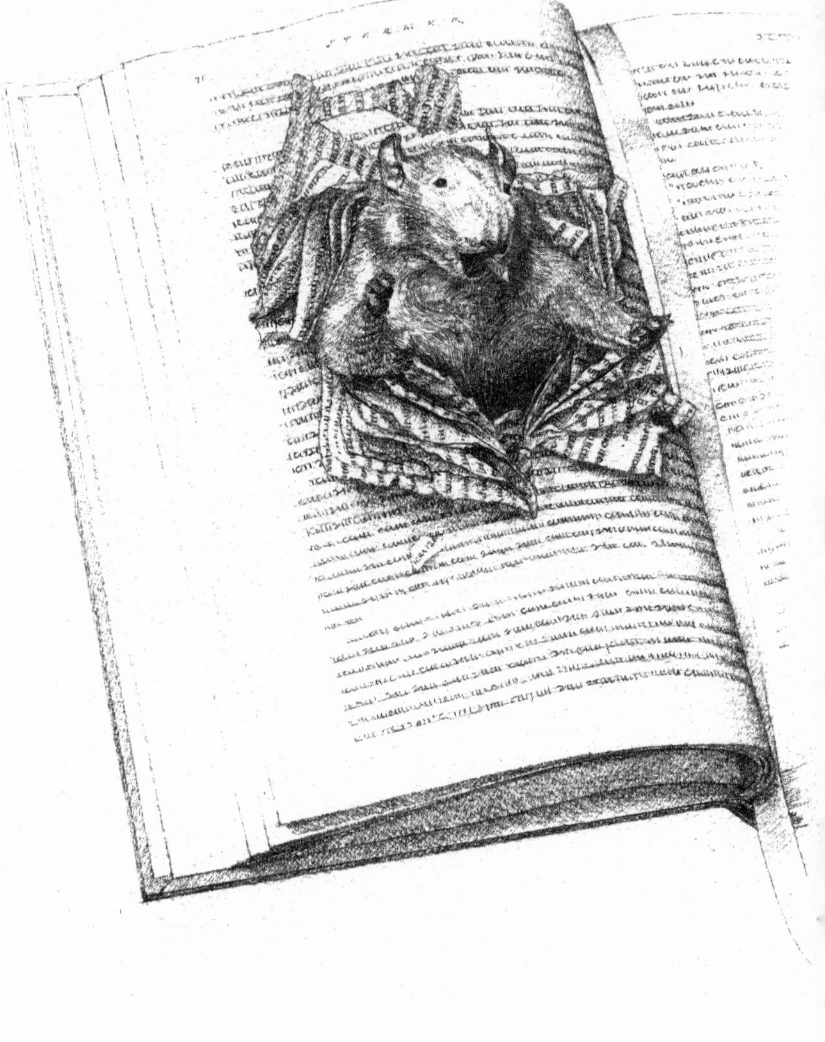

is buckling serves as his bed; recently, he had a nightmare in which he was taught to read.

—François Hébert, *le Dernier Chant de l'avant-dernier dodo* (the last song of the next-to-last dodo)

🐀 Devoured/Devouring

🐀 *I hope the rat remains safely ensconced in his library with Madame de Sévigné, and troubled by nothing more fearsome than an occasional nightmare, for the world is full of savage and voracious beings, even ones with branches and leaves. This particular tree nicely prefigures the Spanish vampire that's the object of pursuit in* Natural History, *by Joan Perucho, a Catalan who also wrote about art and pleasures at the table, and a member of Spain's National Academy of Gastronomy.*

At this moment, they felt a strange vibration that seemed to come from a nearby tree whose foliage was exceptionally dense and luxuriant. Its branches began to sway and droop as the vibrations grew more violent. Novau leapt from his cane chair.

"It's feeding time," our gentleman calmly announced. "It's an unusual species of carnivorous tree.

Don't be alarmed. It was a great effort to acclimatize it here. . . ."

As he uttered these words, Antoni de Montpalau gracefully clapped his hands and Silveri, the footman in charge of the plants, appeared. He was carrying a big cage full of sewer rats, all squeaking furiously.

Silveri opened the cage at a slight distance from the trunk and cautiously stepped back. The rats staggered forth, stupefied by the vibrations, and the voracious branches immediately closed over them. Not one escaped. The tree slowly resumed its original posture and, having digested the rats, opened its leaves, from which some small skeletons the color of old ivory tumbled.

Considering that trees turn into books, imagine the ones created of fibers from this carnivore! And did that carnivore eat crows? Our ravenous muse's mother is getting out her handkerchief, to say nothing of his fiancée. Is there a moral along this treacherous path? He who eats books will also be eaten by them. Oh, lovely, libidinal fate! Oh, literated state of grace!

The Grammared Gazebo, with Vampire

Sheltered from the full moon in the Gargantuan gazebo, the transitive vampire and the professor supped together till dawn. "What a distasteful meal!" the vampire hissed, spitting out a sentence fragment on which she had nearly choked, and smoothing down her skirt. Her host disdained a passive voice on his plate, then had second thoughts, set it in the middle of the table, and tickled it till it danced. A succulent bit of action resulted, reminiscent in texture of calamari or well-muscled prose. Some killer apostrophes scuttled across the floor and whimpered in the corner like Gregor Samsa, after being hurled from the repast in disgust.

The professor nibbled on a possessive pronoun and toasted his finicky guest with a goblet of ink. "Ink: the juice of the dread revolver," the vampire quoted from a Surrealist poem he neither knew nor liked. "You have lost your new gnu, unfortunately," he replied, lifting the statement out of his own book. "No, my nude gnu is in the closet," she quipped. As the night wore on, and the host's eyelids grew heavy, he roused himself to gnaw distractedly on the bones of linguistic structure, wishing she'd have the grace to leave, but she lingered on, sucking the marrow out of a heap of overused, exhausted, deracinated words that had to suffice for dessert.

—Anika Copulescu

𝒪 *This particular vampire is a slight deviant from her species, but I am convinced that one reason the vampire holds such eternal appeal and fascination for us is that it embodies pure desire. We admire the desire, identify with it, wishing we could be so free of ambivalence, and it's also nice for us to feel so wanted. The very idea of a vampire with an eating disorder is preposterous!*

𝒪 Food in a Frame

𝒪 *In one way or another I am saying or showing, on every page of this book, that literature and art are nourishing, more than merely snacks. Marcel Aymé's story "la Bonne Peinture" takes this certitude to new heights, on the slopes of Montmartre:*

By the time he had reached the age of thirty-five his painting had become so rich, so sensitive, so solid that it afforded true nourishment not only to the spirit but to the flesh as well. The beholder had but to gaze attentively at one of his canvases for some twenty or thirty minutes and it was as though he had eaten a meal consisting (for example) of *paté en croute,* roast chicken and fried potatoes, camembert, *crème au chocolat* and assorted fruits washed down by a sound St. Emilion.

The painter Lafleur finds even his meat ration is too much for him; he is never hungry, yet puts on weight, glows with health—so much so that Hermèce, his dealer, fears Lafleur has come into some money and will raise his prices. On visiting Lafleur's studio for the first time since this phenomenon began, Hermèce too is overcome by the spreading pleasure of these gastronomic effects:

Hermèce felt a wave of warmth rising on his face. His cheeks flushed, his ears tingled and his flesh grew heavy with a sense of well-being. First he loosened his tie, then he unbuttoned his waistcoat and finally he loosened his belt.

Wrapping up one painting to take with him, arranging for the others to be called for the following day, Hermèce is taking his leave:

"I'm meeting Bonnier on the Place du Tertre and he's taking me home to dinner in his car. The curious thing is, I seem to have lost my appetite completely, although when I met you I was feeling ravenous."

Naturally, as the fable proceeds, gluttony prevails, and the poor do not profit from these framed cafés.

Aymé translates the system of postwar food rations into another solution for not enough work, money, food to go around in "The Life-Ration," where citizens, according to their usefulness to society, are granted only a certain number of days each month to be actually present in their lives.

Of Chopsticks and Evanescence

Ruby Wang's was a Chinese restaurant in a dirty brick building just a block from the dust and decrepitude of Washington Square. There was an air of great fragility in the Ruby Wang restaurant. The chairs and tables were of a splintering bamboo, and the menu was scrawled on a cobweb-thin paper. The dishes were nearly weightless in their eggshell-like texture. Even the food had a flavor of dejected evanescence.* Thomas Wolfe's enormous body and low, grumbling voice made the cutlery look like trinkets in a brittle Lilliput. . . .

The waitress brought our lunch, along with some chopsticks.

"Would you like to use the chopsticks, gentlemen? Or would you boys prefer forks?"

"I'll try chopsticks," said Wolfe after a sultry hesitation, during which his eyes fixed on the rice with alarm.

The waitress brought the chopsticks and Wolfe attacked the rice, which eluded his chopsticks with insectlike dexterity. He kept poking at the rice with a feverish determination while small drops of sweat exploded on his forehead.

—Frederic Prokosch, *Voices*

---

* Emily Dickinson would have fared quite well here, and tickled the dejection as she toyed with her food: "I would eat evanescence slowly."

ℛ Anarchy and the Everlasting Question

Unparalleled cunning, great honesty of thought, and
intelligence sharpened to a degree, will be required to
enable man to escape from his stiff exterior and suc-
ceed in better reconciling order with disorder, form
with the formless, maturity with eternal and sacred im-
maturity. In the meantime, tell me which you prefer,
red peppers or fresh cucumbers?

—Witold Gombrowicz

ℛ *In this same novel, Gombrowicz's* Ferdydurke, *the narrator-
protagonist abuses, embellishes (with bread crumbs, salt
and pepper, two toothpicks) and demolishes a fruit salad
to assert his identity with a young lady and her parents,
then eats his creation of destruction with great obvious
enjoyment, even the toothpicks:*

No, the battle was not yet won, but at least I had recov-
ered the power to act. Just as I had made a mess of the
fruit salad, reduced it to anarchy and disorder, so could
I wreck the schoolgirl's modernism, stuff her with
strange and heterogeneous things, and corrupt her by

them. Forward against the modern style, against the beauty of the modern schoolgirl! But softly, softly . . .

🙠 *Gombrowicz's entry in his journal greatly pleases our muse, who would apply these words to many a literary fête. (Besides, the skeleton is pleasantly occupied, in Raymond Queneau's* The Bark Tree, *with a piece of bread.)*

What a bore is the everlasting question: What did you mean by *Ferdydurke?* Come, come, be more sensuous, less cerebral, start dancing with the book instead of asking for meanings. Why take so much interest in the skeleton if it's got a body?

In Herbis, et in Verbis:
Stuffed Mirror

Me and my books in the same apartment:
like a gherkin in its vinegar.

—Gustave Flaubert

In an age when just the composition of a salad required
a great knowledge of herbs, their flavours and combined tastes, it was commonly said that "In herbis, et in
verbis et in lapidibus sunt virtutes" ("There are powers
in herbs, words, and stones"). The syncretic character
of late medieval cuisine . . . finds a mirror-like reflec-
tion in the taste for farce and linguistic blending, and
in the interweaving and overlapping of words. Farce,
whether "stuffed" or "mixed," makes up the combination of seasoned ingredients which conspire to please
the palate; it is the dietary archetype at the origin of
linguistic structuring and presides over the stuffing of
vocabulary and locutions.

—Piero Camporesi, *Bread of Dreams*

Aunt Lettuce, I want to look under your skirt.

—Charles Simic

About farce, the dramatic comedy genre: it does come from the word for stuffing, which is what it's made of—overloaded plot, exaggerated characters, copulating coincidences.

Rossini took one look at a cannelloni and decided that stuffing was its destiny. The result was named Cannelloni Rossini—so I learned from an Argentine painter (also inspired in the kitchen and the fireplace) I call El Gaucho Geométrico.

As Cecilia Bartoli divined, Rossini would spend a good deal of time before a deadline enjoying pasta and wines and not composing a single note. See Robert Kelly imagining Rossini, in the nighttime of this book.

 Newsbeat

The Daily Daily

A man clambers onto the streetcar after having bought the daily paper and tucking it under his arm. Half an hour later he gets off, the same newspaper under the same arm.

Only now it's not the same newspaper, now it's a pile of printed sheets which the man drops on a bench in the plaza.

It hardly stays alone a minute on the bench, the pile of printed sheets is converted into a newspaper again when a young boy sees it, reads it, and leaves it converted into a pile of printed sheets.

It sits alone on the bench hardly a minute, the pile of printed sheets converted again into a newspaper when an old woman finds it, reads it, and leaves it changed into a pile of printed sheets. But then she carries it home and on the way home uses it to wrap up a pound of beets, which is what newspapers are fit for after all these exciting metamorphoses.

—Julio Cortázar, *Cronopios and Famas*

The Electric Storm in the Milk Pan

Hold the newsreader's nose squarely, waiter, or friendly milk will countermand my trousers.

—Stephen Fry

Only there are suppressions of sound which are not temporary. The man who has become completely deaf cannot even heat a pan of milk by his bedside without having to keep an eye open to watch, on the tilted lid, for the white hyperborean reflexion, like that of a coming snowstorm . . . ; for already the fitfully swelling egg of the boiling milk is reaching its climax in a series of sidelong undulations, puffs out and fills a few drooping sails that had been puckered by the cream, sending a nacreous spinnaker bellying out in the hurricane, until the cutting off of the current, if the electric storm is exorcised in time, will make them all twirl round on themselves and scatter like magnolia petals. But should the sick man not have been quick enough in taking the necessary precautions, presently, his drowned books and watch scarcely emerging from the milky tidal wave, he will be obliged to call the old nurse, who, though he be himself an eminent statesman or a famous writer,

will tell him that he has no more sense than a child of
five.

—Marcel Proust, *Remembrance of Things Past*

ℛ The Secret Center

ℛ In Pascal Quignard's exquisite novel The Salon in Württemberg, *the narrator's soon-to-be-betrayed and very good
friend Florent Seinecé cultivates and feeds an absolute
passion for candies. Indeed, Charles's first meeting with
him is as an unnoticed voyeur: Seinecé enters the room,
takes a handful of candies out of his pocket, and
arranges them in various configurations: triangles, dia-
mond shapes, and quincunxes, muttering a nonsense song
to himself as he moves them about. Their growing friendship finds them spending weekends together, along with
Seinecé's wife and daughter. For his birthday, after a fabulous ceremony Seinecé performs over his daughter's
wheelbarrow gift (pouring a glass of wine over piles of
grass, invoking the gods, and scattering sugared almonds
and crumbled macaroons), Florent lights into his pres-
ents, which of course include some special candies:*

Neguses—warm soft chocolate centers with a shiny
hard toffee coating rather like the varnish on an
old violin. Lastly came the Lolottes de Nevers—

creamy-textured fruit jellies wearing saris of crystal-lized sugar. . . . What attracted me about them . . . was the notion of putting several layers of sugar around a center—around truth, or despair, or desire, or sin. Can-dies palm a kind of pill off on us, and we feel anxious unless we've identified it with our teeth or tongues. They're like sonatas, theories, religions, love, perhaps even fear—so many layers of varying degrees of sweet-ness or bitterness clothing naked entities themselves of varying degrees of brazenness or crudity. To tell the truth, that's why, though I'm curious about them, I don't really like candies of any kind. I like cakes: they don't conceal any secret. . . . In a way, the rivalry be-tween Seinecé and me, which also bound us together, was a contest between confectionery and pastry.

Still, Charles confesses to a fondness for licorice tins, whose contents interest him only slightly, yet prompt this serpentine description, a confection for the reader, and many years and one reconciliation later, since candies are always present whenever the two men are together, he is further inspired to a devilish, double simile:

I remember some of my friends unfurling funereal black ribbons of licorice in the playground in

Bergheim. . . . Each velvet ribbon was coiled up like an
Egyptian snake, surrounding a kind of pearly button
right in the middle. The whole thing made me think of
a strange curved bow in the end of which the maker
had set a fragment of mother-of-pearl. . . .

I'd brought some marzipan candies called *calissons
d'Aix* . . . *Calissons d'Aix* are one of the candies I like
best, because they're almost pastries and because
they're light in the hand, soft to the teeth, subtle to the
taste, and shaped like mandorlas, the almond-shaped
auras in which Christ appears in representations of the
Last Judgment. Also because in them the tragic apple,
the female apple, the apple of Eden, gradually gives
way to the almond, because they've retained some of
the smell of green cypresses and Mont Sainte-Victoire;
because their whiteness reminds me more of the color
of human skin than milk, canine teeth, or innocence;
because they're a kind of diabolical host, like the little
bits of consecrated bread enclosed in the unleavened
bread of the host, like a gangster's face covered with a
woman's silk stocking.

*Candies (the word is of Persian origin) have plenty of
mouths (and skies!) to fill elsewhere. Sergei Dovlatov
takes the marzipan of Barthes and Quignard, turns it
into an adjective in Russian, and uses it to describe a bu-*

reaucrat in The Compromise: "*. . . an unctuous, marzi-panish person. A certain type: the timid manipulator.*"

"The Conjuror Made Off with the Dish," by Naguib Mahfouz, finds a young boy losing the dish but tasting his first kiss, colored and sweetened by the red and white candies known as "lady's fleas," on which the girl is leisurely sucking when he meets her.

In Virginia Woolf's Mrs. Dalloway, *unconnected characters are linked through their different views of an airplane advertising toffee in the sky:*

Out fluttered behind it a thick ruffled bar of white smoke which curled and wreathed upon the sky in letters. . . . looping, writing a T, an O, an F.

Storms and Bread Crumbs

> I never anticipated that I should carry a ballet-dancer's
> shawl, buy her new gloves, clean her old ones with
> breadcrumbs.*
>
> —Ivan Turgenev, "Correspondences"

Leo Tolstoy and Ivan Turgenev had a very tempestuous
friendship, charted in Tolstoy's diary through all the din-
ners, quarrels, reconciliations, the slinging of epithets.
Turgenev, while working on A Nest of Gentlefolk, *would*
visit Tolstoy at Yasnaya Polyana, roll his eyes at Tol-
stoy's sister Marya, then write his friend Botkin:

> I'm through with Tolstoy. He has ceased to exist for
> me. . . . If I eat a bowl of soup and like it, I know by
> that fact alone and with absolute certainty that Tolstoy
> will find it bad, and vice versa.

---

* Just before the Union of Soviet Socialist Republics ceased to exist,
a cookbook was issued that contained nothing but recipes using
bread crumbs ingeniously.

Tolstoy came to his marriage with no teeth. His cook, Nicolai Mikhailovich, a flautist too, made special dishes for the count. His art as a flautist contributed to one of his more toothsome treats: delicious hot pastries that he made rise by blowing air into them, as if playing his instrument. These pastries were known to the family as the "sighs of Nicolai."

Moscow and the Muse

There were a few young people of indeterminate profession; an old man with a guitar; teenage poets; actors who turned out to be chauffeurs and chauffeurs who turned out to be actors; a demobilized ballerina who was always crying, "Hey, I'll call our gang over, too"; ladies in diamonds; unlicensed jewelers; unattached girls with spiritual aspirations in their eyes; philosophers with unfinished dissertations; a deacon from Novorossisk who always brought a suitcase full of salted fish; and a Tungus from eastern Siberia, who'd got stuck in Moscow—he was afraid the capital's cuisine would spoil his digestion and so would ingest only some kind of fat, which he ate out of a jar with his fingers.

. . . They all considered Grishunya a genius; a collection of his verse had been on the verge of publication for years, but a certain pernicious Makushkin, on whom everything depended, was blocking it— Makushkin, who had sworn that only over his dead body . . . They cursed Makushkin, extolled Grishunya, the women asked him to read more, more. Flushed, self-conscious, Grisha read on—thick, significant poems that recalled expensive, custom-made cakes covered with ornamental inscriptions and triumphant meringue towers, poems slathered with sticky linguistic icing, poems containing abrupt, nutlike crunches of clustered sounds and excruciating, indigestible caramel confections of rhyme. "Eh-eh-eh," said the Tungus, shaking his head; apparently he didn't understand a word of Russian. "What's wrong? Doesn't he like it?" murmured the other guests. "No, no—I'm told that's the way they express praise," said Agniya, fluffing her hair nervously, afraid that the Tungus would jinx her.

—Tatyana Tolstaya, "The Poet and the Muse,"
Sleepwalker in a Fog

Breakfast with a Barber in Petersburg and the fresh hot roll with horrible contents

An incredible thing happened in Petersburg on March 25th. Ivan Yakovlevich, the barber on Voznesensky Avenue (his last name has been lost and does not even figure on the signboard bearing a picture of a gentleman with a soapy cheek and the inscription WE ALSO LET BLOOD HERE), woke up rather early and detected a smell of newly baked bread. He raised himself a little and saw that his wife, a quite respectable woman and one extremely fond of coffee, was taking fresh rolls out of the oven.

"Praskovia Osipovna," he said to his wife, "no coffee for me this morning. I'll have a hot roll with onions instead."

Actually Ivan Yakovlevich would have liked both but he knew his wife frowned on such whims. And, sure enough, she thought:

"It's fine with me if the fool wants bread. That'll leave me another cup of coffee."

And she tossed a roll onto the table.

Mindful of his manners, Ivan Yakovlevich put his frock coat on over his nightshirt, seated himself at the table, poured some salt, got a couple of onions, took a knife and, assuming a dignified expression, proceeded to cut the roll in two.

Suddenly he stopped, surprised. There was something whitish in the middle of the roll. He poked at it with his knife, then felt it with his finger.

"It's quite compact," he muttered under his breath. "Whatever can it be?"

He thrust in two fingers this time and pulled it out. It was a nose.

He almost fell off his chair. Then he rubbed his eyes and felt the thing again. It was a nose all right, no doubt about it. And, what's more, a nose that had something familiar about it. His features expressed intense horror.

But the intensity of the barber's horror was nothing compared with the intensity of his wife's indignation.

"Where," she screamed, "did you lop off that nose, you beast? You crook," she shouted, "you drunkard! I'll report you to the police myself, you thug! Three customers have complained to me before this about the way you keep pulling their noses when you shave them, so that it's a wonder they manage to stay on at all."

But Ivan Yakovlevich, at that moment more dead than alive, was immune to her attack. He had remembered where he had seen the nose before and it was on none other than Collegiate Assessor Kovalev, whom he shaved regularly each Wednesday and Sunday.

"Wait, my dear, I'll wrap it in a rag and put it away somewhere in a corner. Let it stay there for a while, then I'll take it away."

"I won't even listen to you! Do you really imagine that I'll allow a cut-off nose to remain in my place, you old crumb! All you can do is strop your damn razor and when it comes to your duties, you're no good. You stupid, lousy, skirt-chasing scum! So you want me to get into trouble with the police for your sake? Is that it, you dirty mug? You're a stupid log, you know. Get it out of here. Do what you like with it, you hear me, but don't let me ever see it here again."

The barber stood there dumbfounded. He thought and thought but couldn't think of anything.

"I'll be damned if I know how it happened," he said in the end, scratching behind his ear. "Was I drunk last night when I came home? I'm not sure. Anyway, it all sounds quite mad: bread is a baked product while a nose is something else again. Makes no sense to me . . ."

So he fell silent. The thought that the police would find the nose on him and accuse him drove him to despair. He could already see the beautiful silver-braided, scarlet collars of the police and started trembling all over.

—Nikolai Gogol, "The Nose"

Like a Tea-Tray in the Sky

It was at a tea party in Petersburg, not Wonderland, that Gogol heard an anecdote that inspired "The Overcoat." But he would have been a welcome guest at "A Mad Tea-Party," although the dormouse might have raised sleepy objections when Gogol pulled his nose.

> *Twinkle, twinkle, little bat!*
> *How I wonder what you're at!*
> *Up above the world you fly,*
> *Like a tea-tray in the sky.*

—Lewis Carroll, *Alice's Adventures in Wonderland*

The Hatter opened his eyes very wide on hearing this; but all he *said* was "Why is a raven like a writing desk?"

So the muse will come and mate with it, of course.

He was the kind of man who kept a diagram showing where you sat when you dined with him and what you ate, lest he serve you the same dish when you came again.

—Alexander Woollcott on Lewis Carroll

He was also the kind of man who knew how to throw a tea party for eternity, for his Mad Tea-Party continues in the collective imagination. No one who reads that scene of dirty dishes, swapped insults and non sequiturs, and tenuous places at table ever really leaves: its endlessness is as assured as the lingering image of a disappearing-down-to-his-last-grin-and-whiskers Cheshire Cat. And why should this author not be cautious about what he serves his guests, and where? Every time Alice puts something in her mouth, she is alarmingly transformed, and transported besides: a sudden change in the scenery and company always accompanies the change in her size.

$\mathcal{R}$ World without Me Cake

There are no moments happier than those I experience when on Sunday morning I enter a pastry shop to buy a cake.

I selected a small pastry shop for this weekly rite. In the large ones there are too many customers, whereas the lane on which this particular shop is located is very good: it is uncrowded, with slightly bluish slabs of granite in the sidewalk and, in front of one of the houses, a wonderful fence whose design is like the handwriting of some famous person who lived long ago; but, above all, that lane is associated for me with an amazing sensation which visits me sometimes and which I call "the world without me" . . .

The salesgirls already know me. From all sides curly bright little heads nod to me. It is like entering a greenhouse: suddenly through a clear space in the green undergrowth you see the swaying head of a snake or some marvelous flower . . . It is the same way here, only the undergrowth is replaced by boxes and vases. And there is the same stuffy, slightly poisonous, wicked atmosphere. . . . As always, I take a strawberry cake. . . .

Her small hand, its little fingers poised in the direction of the cake, swims among the masses of confectionary. With the aid of the other hand, which had swum up in the same way, she removes the cake, and there it is in front of me, that strawberry cake which looks to me like something from a fairy tale or like a fairy's friend.

—Yury Olesha, *No Day without a Line*

Balzac Laments, the Bride Rejoices: Coffee!

Alexander Pope, who had a constant headache during the long disease his life, used to sniff coffee all day long and nights in public houses to relieve the pulsing pain. Like alcohol, coffee is a social drink: people are always asking, "Do you want a cup of coffee?" when they mean, "I wanna drag you to my bed." Coffee is also a necessary ritual between the sheets and the streets. Bach wrote a piece called "The Coffee Cantata," whose raucous laughter and jollity we can only attribute to the magic of the drug. It's about a father who won't let his daughter marry unless she gives up drinking coffee, but she outsmarts the old man and has coffee written into the marriage articles, and becomes the first bride in history to live happily ever after.

—Karen Elizabeth Gordon, *The Red Shoes*

The magic of the drug was sadly slipping away from Honoré de Balzac's enjoyment and use of it long before he died of caffeine poisoning. "It now excites my brain for only fifteen days consecutively," he lamented to a friend. His output, still, was stupendous, and done on little sleep. Initially it was hunger that drove Balzac to seek sustenance and stimulation in his lovely, lethal coffeepot—which you can see for yourself when you visit his house in placid Passy. Hidden from his creditors, here he lived under the name of Madame de Breugnol, correcting and writing many of his major works. Friends coming to visit had to ask for him by this name, adding a code phrase such as "The season of plums has arrived" or "I bring laces from Belgium," which assured their admission to Balzac's hospitality. In contrast to soirées of the booed writers' dinner and Turgenev's crowd cooked for by Stepan, Balzac's dinners were of the simplest fare, accompanied by cheap acrid wines dressed up in labels of the grandest names and exalted by Balzac's eloquence about their bogus vintages. Honoré de Balzac deserves special honor in this book for having written all his human comedy with a crow's quill, or the quills of many crows. To alleviate the pain the aforementioned demise must have caused you, I'll leave you with an original breakfast (with coffee) from The Princess Hoppy, *whose shameless relatives you'll meet again in the screening room.*

Thus, one Sunday, at eight on the dotted dot, North Dakota, King Desmond's trusted dromedary, entered the Royal Bedroom, balancing the breakfast tray on his hump: coffee, marmalade and melted licorice toasts for the King—tea sweetened with litchis and Turkish delight, tarama followed by moussaka for Queen Ingrid.

—Jacques Roubaud,
The Princess Hoppy or the Tale of Labrador

℘ The Charm of the Forbidden Teapot, with Dessert

The Armenian language cannot be worn out; its boots are stone. Well, certainly, the thick-walled word, the layers of air in the semi-vowels. But is that all there is to its charm? No! Where does its traction come from? How to explain it? Make sense of it?

I felt the joy of pronouncing sounds forbidden to Russian lips, secret sounds, outcast, and perhaps, on some deep level, shameful.

There was some fine water boiling in a pewter teapot and suddenly a pinch of marvelous black tea was thrown into it.

That's how I felt about the Armenian language.

—Osip Mandelstam, *Journey to Armenia*

I just stood there in the shop, not coping very well with this decisiveness voiced in such an indecisive, undulating language, like food that may be filling but is unappetizing. Actually, the Hungarian had mastered my language rather well, but at the end of every sentence he would add for dessert a Hungarian word that I couldn't understand.

—Milorad Pavić, *Dictionary of the Khazars*

The Tables Turned

"On days like this even snakes that have venom only
on Fridays become poisonous," Atanas Svilar thought,
listening to his son, to the boy who still adored grapes
hot from the sun and ripe apricots in which you could
almost feel the jam simmering on the branch in the
heat. Atanas Svilar sat there and looked in amazement
at his son, and then at his own hands on either side of
the plate, and he could not recognize them. Two
scalded goose heads peered out from his sleeves and
tried in vain to swallow the knife and fork. . . .

—Milorad Pavić

In July, 1923, Franz Kafka was staying at the vacation
colony of Volksheim, where he was loved and cared for
by Dora Diamant, the cook. Pietro Citati recounts a
dinner given in honor of the author, the guests including a number of intimidated children. One of them,
who was more afraid than the others, got up from the
table to get something, but he stumbled and fell. The
others began to laugh. But before the laughter could
break out further, humiliating the child forever, Kafka
said loudly in a tone of ardent admiration: "How well
you fell! And how magnificently you got up!"

—Salim Jay, *les Écrivains sont dans leur assiette*

§ *The tables also knocked. At the Place des Vosges these days, you may cast your eyes upon the table in Victor Hugo's Chinese dining room where séances once took place.*

§ The Taste of the Text

The linguistic philosophers of France, especially the late Roland Barthes, understood how French cuisine and French culture are related, and how both fit with structuralist philosophy. A Parisian dinner is meant to be a single elegant statement, like a well-turned sentence or an outfit from Yves Saint-Laurent. The Anglo-Saxon view of a banquet can be expressed in terms of the history of the world. You begin with soup—water with things swimming in it—then move on to the aqueous kingdom, then to flying creatures, then to mammals. Finally you celebrate man in cheeses and desserts, both products of sophisticated culture. This is the diachronic view, which the French reject. They prefer to see the various courses as syntagms, or sentence components—soup adjective, fish noun, chicken adverb.

—Anthony Burgess, "The Language of Food" in
Homage to Qwert Yuiop

. . . is not a good wine the wine whose flavor oscillates, alters, doubles, so that the mouthful swallowed does not have quite the same taste as the next mouthful taken? In the draught of good wine, as in the taking of the text, there is a torsion, a twist of degrees: it turns back, like a lock of hair.

—Roland Barthes, "La Fraisette"
in *Roland Barthes by Roland Barthes*

Pastry in Perspective

The fine arts are five in number, namely: painting, sculpture, poetry, music, and architecture, the principal branch of the latter being pastry.

—Antonin Carême

This is no small jest. Remember that architects must build maquettes, models, which require some of the same fine eye and hand movements, the same precision as the confection of a pastry. Carême's words came true shortly after I had first encountered them: an architect I have known since childhood, upon retiring, enrolled in pastry-making school and now supplies several Bay Area restaurants with his sugared constructions.

Metaphysical Cocoa

Look, there's no metaphysics on earth like chocolate.
—Fernando Pessoa

In Mexico, they beat it in water to make it foam, and the ladies of the New World not only consumed it all day long at home but also drank it in church. Their confessors began by chastising them before they wound up joining them in this habit. As Alexandre Dumas writes in his Dictionnaire de cuisine, *"Finally, Father Escobar, whose metaphysics were as subtle as his morality was accommodating, formally declared that chocolate made with water did not break any fast." Upon its arrival in Spain in the seventeenth century, it was an instant hit with the women and monks, and soon became quite the fashion. Piero Camporesi has devoted a dazzling book to the role of chocolate in the literary salons and thought trends of the eighteenth century, when women ruled the life of the mind and cultivated a lighter, airier cuisine in which the drink of chocolate was a bass note and a star.*

Powdered sugar, the white gold of candy and pastry makers, gave rise to the large breads of Holland . . .

softer and silkier than the Venetian sugared breads. *The century of the woman* doted on chocolate, celebrated in prose and in verse, adored the sugar which, worked upon by the architect–pastry chefs, left its imprint on the retina and ran down the throat in the form of rosolios, syrups, sherbets, gelatins, conserves, in confections of fruits and flowers, in the undulating volutes of iced sugar "so pretty to look upon," in the polychrome decorations of dessert. A sugared, velvety fever took over the patrician palaces and houses of Jesuits. The epoch of chocolate and sugar had found among the brothers of Saint Ignatius of Loyola their most adoring devotees and their most fervent songsters.

—Piero Camporesi, *le Goût du chocolat*

A Dumas Scenario, with George Sand for Breakfast

14 September 1863

Dinner at Magny's. Afterwards, Sainte-Beuve left us drinking the mixture of rum and curaçao he always prepares for us at dessert.

"By the way, Gautier, you are just back from Madame Sand's at Nohant, aren't you? Is it amusing?"

"As amusing as a Moravian monastery! I arrived in the evening. It's a long way from the station. They left my box in a bush. . . . They gave me dinner. The food's good, but there's too much game and chicken, and that doesn't suit me. There was Marechal, the painter, there and Alexandre Dumas *fils* and Madame Calamatta."

"And how's Dumas *fils?* Still ill?"

"Oh, terribly unhappy. You know what he does these days? He sits down in front of a sheet of paper and stays there for four hours. He writes three lines. He goes off to have a cold bath or do some exercises . . . then he comes back and decides that his three lines are damn stupid."

"Well, that shows some sense!" said somebody.

"And then he crosses out everything except three words. Every now and then his father arrives from Naples and says: 'Get me a cutlet and I'll finish your play for you,' writes the scenario, brings in a whore, borrows some money and goes off again. Dumas *fils* reads the scenario, likes it, goes and has a bath, reads the scenario again, decides that it's stupid, and spends a year revising it. And when his father comes back, he finds the same three words from the same three lines as the year before!"

"And what sort of life do they lead at Nohant?"

"You breakfast at ten. On the last stroke, when the hand is exactly at ten o'clock, everybody sits down without waiting for Mme Sand, who arrives looking like a sleepwalker and stays asleep throughout the meal."

—Edmond and Jules de Goncourt,
Pages from the Goncourt Journal

The Romantic Cigar

"All this happened several years ago," said Baron d'Ormesan. "One of my friends gave me a box of Havanas which he recommended to me specially because they were of the same quality as those the late King of England could not do without.

"That evening, when I opened the lid, I was delighted by the exquisite aroma which proceeded from those marvellous cigars. I compared them in my mind to well-stacked shells in an arsenal. Arsenal of peace! Shells invented in fortunate dreams to defeat boredom! Then, having delicately removed one of the cigars from the box, I decided that my comparison with shells was not apt. Rather, it resembled the finger of a Negro, and the ring of gold paper round it increased this illusion, which its beautiful brown colour had suggested to me. I pierced the cigar with loving care, lit it, and began to draw the smoke beatifically in large aromatic puffs.

"After a few seconds, however, a most disagreeable

taste was all that came to my mouth; the smoke from my cigar seemed to have the aroma of burned paper.

" 'The King of England appears to have had a less refined taste in tobacco than I would have expected,' I said to myself. 'It is possible, after all, that fraud, so widespread in our times, did not even spare the palate and throat of Edward VII. Everything is going to the devil. It is no longer possible even to smoke a decent cigar.'

"Making a face, I stopped smoking mine, which without a doubt smelled of burned cardboard. I examined it for a moment, thinking:

" 'Since the Americans now have the upper hand in Cuba, the prosperity of the island may have increased, but Havana cigars are obviously no longer smokeable. The Yankees have probably applied modern methods of culture to the tobacco plantations; the cigar-rollers have certainly been replaced by machines. All this is perhaps more economical, and quicker, but the cigar loses much in the process. Moreover, the one I have just tried to smoke gives me reason to believe that the falsifiers, too, have their fingers in the pie, and that old newspapers dipped in nicotine now take the place of tobacco leaves in the manufacture of Havanas.'

"I was at this point in my reflections when I took the cigar to pieces in order to examine its contents. I was not very surprised to discover, inserted in such a manner as not to prevent the cigar from drawing, a piece of paper which I hastily unrolled. It consisted of a sheet so folded as to protect a small sealed envelope that bore the following address:

Sr. Don José Hurtado y Barral,
Calle de Los Angeles,
Habana

"On the piece of paper, the top edge of which was slightly discoloured by burning, I read with amazement a few lines written in a feminine hand in Spanish, of which the following is a translation:

Imprisoned against my will in the convent of La Merced, I beg the good Christian who happens to investigate this bad cigar to send the attached letter to the address given.

"Astonished, and deeply moved, I took my hat and, having added my address as sender to the envelope, in order that, in the event it did not reach its destination, it would be returned to me, I went out and posted the letter. Then I returned home and lit a second cigar. It was excellent, as were the others. My friend was not mistaken. The King of England knew his Havana tobacco very well.

"I had completely forgotten this romantic incident

when, five or six months later, my servant announced the visit of a Negro couple, both beautifully dressed, who asked me to be so good as to receive them, adding that I did not know them, and that their name would doubtless mean nothing to me.

"I was very intrigued as I entered my drawing room, into which this exotic couple had been shown.

"The Negro gentleman introduced himself with easy assurance, expressing himself in very intelligible French:

" 'I am Don José Hurtado y Barral. . . .'

" 'What! It is you, at last?' I cried with astonishment, suddenly remembering the episode of the cigar.

"But I must admit that it would never have occurred to me that the Havana Romeo and his Juliet were Negroes.

" 'I am he.'

"And he presented his companion, adding:

" 'This is my wife. She has become so, thanks to your kindness. Unsympathetic parents had shut her in a convent in which the nuns made cigars all day long, destined exclusively for the Papal court and that of England.'

"I could not believe it. Hurtado y Barral continued:

" 'We both belong to rich Negro families. There are a certain number of us in Cuba. Though you may not believe it, colour prejudice exists among Negroes just as it does among whites.

" 'The parents of my Dolores wished her at all costs to marry a white man. They hoped above all for a Yankee son-in-law, and, furious because of her determination to marry me, they had her shut up, with the greatest secrecy, in the convent of La Merced.

" 'Not knowing where to find Dolores, I was in despair and ready to kill myself when the letter you had the goodness to send me restored my courage. I abducted my fiancée from the convent, and since then she has become my wife. . . .

" 'You will understand, sir, we would have been ungrateful indeed had we not chosen to visit Paris for our honeymoon; it was also our duty to come and thank you.

" 'I am the owner of one of the largest cigar factories in Havana, and, wishing to make amends for the bad cigar you smoked through our fault, I shall send you twice a year a supply of choice cigars. I have waited only to consult your taste before dispatching the first shipment.'

"Don José had learned his French in New Orleans, and his wife also spoke without an accent, since she had been brought up in France. . . ."

—Guillaume Apollinaire, "The False Amphion"

An Orgy in the Screening Room

The Princess Hoppy or The Tale of Labrador *feeds its characters* such food as vegetable elk, gooseberry boutifara, and a small dessert made of inadequacy jam with a drop of illicit liquor, although the kisses of the princess seem more necessary to the health and sustenance of her uncles and dog than these dinners and the jams that the queens are potting while the kings are plotting and the author is plotting his mathematically sound, linguistically adventurous tale.*

We glue our eyes to the porthole, the better to see what King Desmond, Queen Adirondac and young Brigid, the pink California crane, are doing, at four o'clock in the afternoon, on three deck chairs, in the cabin of King Desmond's yacht. So, what *are* they doing?

---

* These characters deserve mention by name—at least a handful of the almost immediate family: King Imogène, King Babylas, King Eleonor (without an e), Queen Botswanna (born Yolanda and Ygrometria), Queens Eleonore (with an e) and Ingrid—plus the camels North Dakota and South Dakota, and ducks doubling as boats called *doats*. The dog, his place so assured, his identity so intact, has no need of a name.

They are eating a giant strawberry sundae drenched in melted marshmallow with boysenberry syrup, crowned with a high peak of pink whipped cream from "Chantilly, Pennsylvania," and studded with frozen raspberries. Desmond is attacking it from the top with his wooden spoon, Brigid and Adirondac, each on her own side with their fingers! Their faces are distorted by greediness; the spoon and fingers never stop penetrating ever further inside the creamy mass of the sundae, while the boysenberry syrup and the melted marshmallow run down their wrists, down their cheeks and into their eyes! Their eyes are glued to the screen and on this screen a strangely similar scene is taking place: another immense strawberry sundae, absolutely similar to the first one, is giving way before an attack by the spoon and fingers of some characters caught by the camera. Who can these people be? We get as close as possible and we recognize . . .****, the famous oil tycoon, the beautiful Ava G.; and the third (for there are three characters on the screen, as there are three in the cabin), the third is that young slim pink child, as pink as the pink ice cream, as pink as whipped cream from Chantilly, Pennsylvania? Yes, you've guessed right: none other than Brigid, who has come straight from California with her film, in which, by the way, if one were to look closely at the background (the scene shown in the cabin of a yacht anchored in a Sunset

Boulevard swimming pool), one could see another screen in which the pink Brigid is licking another giant strawberry sundae in the company of the Pr . . . of U . . . and the Queen of En . . . what? no? . . . do excuse the tale, but strong pressure is being applied to it not to divulge these names, for security reasons.

The last notes of "There Are No Flies on Auntie" die inside the wax of the record, the last pink spoonfuls of ice cream disappear between sated lips. With a sad movement of the head, we remove our eye from the porthole before it remains glued to it and we leave behind us, far away, King Desmond's yacht.

How innocent nature appears: the sun shines; the river runs, trembling with light. The salmon meditates.

—Jacques Roubaud,
The Princess Hoppy or The Tale of Labrador

Night of Infernal Debauch

Margarita's head began to spin with the fumes of the wine, and she was just about to move on when the cat staged one of his tricks in the swimming pool. Behemoth made a few magic passes in front of Neptune's mouth; immediately all the champagne drained out of the pool, and Neptune began spewing forth a stream of brown liquid. Shrieking with delight the women screamed, "Brandy!" In a few seconds the pool was full.

Spinning around three times like a top, the cat leaped into the air and dived into the turbulent sea of brandy. It crawled out, spluttering, its tie soaked, the gilding gone from its whiskers, and minus its lorgnette. . . .

They seemed to take wing, and in their flight Margarita first saw great stone tanks full of oysters, then a row of hellish furnaces blazing away beneath the glass floor and attended by a frantic crew of diabolic chefs. In the confusion she remembered a glimpse of dark caverns lit by candles where girls were serving meat that sizzled on glowing coals and revelers drank Margarita's health from vast mugs of beer. Then came polar bears playing accordions and dancing a Russian dance on a stage, a salamander doing conjuring tricks unharmed by the flames around it. . . .

—Mikhail Bulgakov, *The Master and Margarita*

Ramzan

. . . Ramzan, a lunar thing, never arrives at the same point of time each year, coming instead with an aura of slight and pleasing dislocation. Somehow it always took us by surprise: new moons are startling to see, even by accident, and Ramzan's moon betokened a month of exquisite precision about the way we were to parcel out our time. On the appointed evenings we would rake the twilight for that possible sliver, and it made the city and body both shudder with expectation to spot that little slip of a moon that signified Ramzan and made the sky historical. How busy Lahore would get! Its minarets hummed, its municipalities pulled out their old air-raid sirens to make the city noisily cognizant: the moon had been sighted, and the fast begun.

I liked it, the waking up an hour before dawn to eat the prefast meal and chat in whispers. For three wintry seasons I would wake up with Dadi, my grandmother, and Ifat and Shahid: we sat around for hours making jokes in the dark, generating a discourse of unholy comradeship. The food itself, designed to keep the penitent sustained from dawn till dusk, was insistent in its richness and intensity, with bread dripping clarified butter, and curried brains, and cumin eggs, and peculiarly potent vermicelli, soaked overnight in sugar and fatted milk. And if I liked the getting up at dawn, then

Dadi completely adored the eating of it all. I think she fasted only because she so enjoyed the *sehri* meal and that mammoth infusion of food at such an extraordinary hour. At three in the morning the rest of us felt squeamish about linking the deep sleep dreams we had just conducted and so much grease—we asked instead for porridge—but Dadi's eating was a sight to behold and admire. She hooted when the city's sirens sounded to tell us that we should stop eating and that the fast had now begun: she enjoyed a more direct relation with God than did petty municipal authorities and was fond of declaiming what Muhammad himself had said in her defense. He apparently told one of his contemporaries that *sehri* did not end until a white thread of light described the horizon and separated the landscape from the sky. In Dadi's book that thread could open into quite an active loom of dawning: the world made waking sounds, the birds and milkmen all resumed their proper functions, but Dadi's regal mastication— on the last brain now—declared it still was night.

—Sara Suleri, *Meatless Days*

Before the Bachot: Eating Words

From the headmaster of Lycée Louis-Le-Grand, Paris, to Monsieur Aupick, the stepfather of Charles Baudelaire

Paris, April 18, 1839

Sir,

This morning your son, summoned by the Assistant-Director to relinquish a note that one of his schoolmates had just slipped to him, refused to give it up, tore it to pieces, and swallowed it. When he was sent to me, he declared that he preferred any punishment to revealing his classmate's secret and, when I urged him to explain further, for the sake of his friend, whom he has now left open to the worst suspicions, he replied with a derisive laugh, the impertinence of which I need not tolerate. I am therefore returning you this young man, who has been endowed with quite exceptional abilities, but who has marred everything through his bad character, which has more than once jeopardized school order. . . .

The Schoolmaster
PIERROT
—Charles Baudelaire: Letters from His Youth

And so young Charles, already developing his spleen—his muse—writing art and literary criticism as well as poetry, had to go to another lycée to pass his baccalauréat, for the abject letter of apology he wrote the schoolmaster did not have the desired effect, not even in beseeching the schoolmaster for lenience so as to spare his mother distress.

Poems to Eat, Poems for Keeps

I make poems which I recite to myself, which I taste, which I play with. I feel no need to communicate them to anyone, even to people I like a lot. I don't write them down. It's so good to daydream, to stammer around something which remains a secret for oneself. It's a sin of gluttony.

—Blaise Cendrars

The poet advises: "Read me. Read me again."
He does not always come away unscathed from
his page, but like the poor, he knows how to
make use of an olive's eternity.

—René Char

CR *Lawrence Durrell is well acquainted with that eternity of olives. He describes the taste in* Prospero's Cell:

A taste older than meat, older than wine.
A taste as old as cold water.

CR *In the Paris of Erik Satie and Blaise Cendrars, the Divan Japonais, a cabaret that published its own review,* La Lanterne Japonaise, *was run by a Lyonnais named Jean Sarrazin (meaning buckwheat), whom everyone called "the olive poet." The name followed him from the days when he'd peddled olives in cafés, the olives wrapped in scraps of paper on which he'd written his own poems.*

ℜ Wayfaring with the Pooka and the Good Fairy

ℜ *In Flann O'Brien's* At Swim-Two-Birds *a birth-bound band of travelers—two cowboys, a demon known as the Pooka, and a Good Fairy—catch the mad king poet Sweeny, badly injured, fallen out of a tree. As they journey onward, they revive him not only with green moss but with extravagant promises of nourishment, so lyrical that they wind up in all manner of song:*

We'll get you a jug of hot punch and a packet of cream crackers with plenty of butter, said Slug, if you'll only walk, if you'll only pull yourself together, man.

And getting around the invalid in a jabbering ring, they rubbed him and cajoled and coaxed, and plied him with honey-talk and long sweet-lilted sentences full of fine words, and promised him metheglin and mugs of viscous tar-black mead thickened with white yeast and the spoils from hives of mountain-bees, and corn-coarse nourishing farls of wheaten bread dipped in musk-scented liquors and sodden with Belgian sherry, an orchard and a swarm of furry honey-glutted bees and a bin of sun-bronzed grain from the granaries of the Orient in every drop as it dripped at the lifting of the hand to the mouth, and inky quids of strong-

smoked tabacca with cherrywood pipes, hubble-dub-
bles, duidins, meerschaums, clays, hickory hookahs and
steel-stemmed pipes with enamel bowls, the lot of
them laid side by side in a cradle of lustrous blue
plush. . . . They also did not hesitate to promise him
sides of hairy bacon, the mainstay and the staff of life
of the country classes, and lamb chops still succulent
with young blood, autumn-heavy yams from venerable
stooping trees, bracelets and garlands of browned
sausages and two baskets of peerless eggs fresh-
collected, a waiting hand under the hen's bottom.
They beguiled him with the mention of salads and
crome custards and the grainy disorder of pulpy boiled
rhubarb, . . . olives and acorns and rabbit-pie, and venison roasted on a smoky spit, and mulatto thick-lipped
delphy cups of black-strong tea. They foreshadowed
the felicity of billowy beds of swansdown carefully laid
crosswise on springy rushes and sequestered with a
canopy of bearskins and generous goatspelts, a couch
for a king with fleshly delectations and fifteen hundred
olive-mellow concubines in constant attendance upon
the hour of desire. Chariots they talked about and dun-
crusted pies exuberant with a sweat of crimson juice,
and tall crocks full of eddying foam-washed stout. . . .
And as they talked, they threaded through the twilight
and the sudden sun-pools of the wild country.

The company continued to travel throughout the
day, pausing at evening to provide themselves with the

sustenance of oakmast and coconuts and with the re-
freshment of pure water from the jungle springs. They
did not cease, either walking or eating, from the de-
lights of colloquy and harmonized talk contrapuntal in
character nor did Sweeny desist for long from stave-
music or from the recital of his misery in verse. On the
brink of night they halted to light faggots with a box of
matches and continued through the tangle and the
grasses with flaming brands above their heads. . . . On
occasion an owl or an awkward beetle or a small coterie
of hedgehogs, attracted by the splendour of the light,
would escort them for a part of the journey until the
circumstances of their several destinations would
divert them again into the wild treachery of the gloom.
The travellers would sometimes tire of the drone of
one another's talk and join together in the metre of
an old-fashioned song, filling their lungs with fly-
thickened air and raising their voices above the sleep-
ing trees. They sang *Home on the Range* and the
pick of the old cowboy airs, the evergreen favorites of
the bunkhouse and the prairie; they joined together
with a husky softness in the lilt of the old come-all-ye's,
the ageless minstrelsy of the native-land, a sob in their
voice as the last note died; they rendered old catches
with full throats, and glees and round-songs and riddle-
me-raddies, *Tipperary* and *Nellie Deane* and *The
Shade of the Old Apple Tree*. They sang Cuban love-
songs and moonsweet madrigals and selections from

the best and the finest of the Italian operas, from the compositions of Puccini and Meyerbeer and Donizetti and Gounod and the Maestro Mascagni as well as an aria from *The Bohemian Girl* by Balfe, and intoned the choral complexities of Palestrina the pioneer. They rendered two hundred and forty-two (242) songs by Schubert in the original German words, and sang a chorus from *Fidelio* (by Beethoven of *Moonlight Sonata* fame) and the *Song of the Flea*, and a long excerpt from a Mass by Bach, as well as innumerable pleasantries from the able pens of no less than Mozart and Handel. To the stars . . . they gave with a thunderous spirit such pieces by Offenbach, Schumann, Saint-Saens and Granville Bantock as they could remember. They sang entire movements from cantatas and oratorios and other items of sacred music, *allegro ma non troppo, largo,* and *andante cantabile.*

They were all so preoccupied with music that they were still chanting spiritedly in the dark undergrowth long after the sun, earlier astir than usual, had cleaned the last vestige of the soiling night from the verdure of the tree-tops—rosy-fingered pilgrim of the sandal grey. When they suddenly arrived to find mid-day in a clearing, they wildly reproached each other with bitter words and groundless allegations of bastardy and low birth as they collected berries and haws into the hollows of their hats against the incidence of a late breakfast.

Happy Birthday, Wittgenstein,
My Favorite Washer of
the Dishes

He liked washing dishes after a meal. He put the dishes
and silverware in the bathtub, studied carefully the de-
tergent, the temperature of the water, and spent hours
at his task, and hours more in the rinsing and drying. If
he was a guest for several days, all the meals had to be
identical with the first, whether breakfast, lunch, or
dinner. What he ate was no matter, just so it was always
the same. . . . When he lay dying of cancer at his doctor's house, the doctor's kind wife remembered his
birthday and baked him a cake. Moreover, she wrote on
it with icing, "Many Happy Returns." When Wittgenstein asked her if she had examined the implications of
that sentiment, she burst into tears and dropped the
cake. "You see," Wittgenstein said to the doctor when
he arrived on the scene, "I have neither the cake nor an
answer to my question."

—Guy Davenport, "Wittgenstein,"
in *The Geography of the Imagination*

◌ Eine Kleine Noshmusik

During a five-year period (1985–1990) nineteen adults came to our center for evaluation of involuntary sleep-related eating. Most patients also reported histories of complex and injurious non-eating nocturnal behaviors, including sleepwalking.

During their sleep-related eating episodes, the majority of the patients binged on high-calorie foods and often prepared entire meals; others ate modest snacks such as cold cereal. Impaired judgment and sloppiness were common, as patients ate raw or cooked food with their hands, poured food on themselves, attempted to drink ammonia cleaning solution, dropped food on the floor, or took items out of the freezer and scattered them around the house. They also indiscriminately put large quantities of sugar or salt on food, and ate butter and sugar by the spoonful.

The impulsive consumption of very hot beverages or oatmeal led to scalding injuries. Several patients lacerated their digits while cutting food. Frenzied running to the kitchen resulted in collisions with furniture, doors, and walls. Disinhibited eating extended to peculiar concoctions having non-nutritive ingredients (e.g., cigarettes).

Dreamlike mental imagery could accompany such

activity, as with one patient who carried lettuce around the house while dreaming of finding a safe place for it. Another patient dressed up for a dinner party and then ate while dreaming that the guests had arrived.

—Carlos H. Schenck, Thomas D. Hurwitz,
Scott R. Bundlie, and Mark W. Mahowald,
"Sleep-Related Eating Disorders," *Sleep*

One More Morsel of This After All Adorable Cosmos: Rossini

Note 4: *a large cookie.* As one sits and hears the last large sumptuous measures of Richard Strauss's *Capriccio*, his last opera, written and performed (in the recording heard now) while the world was burning down around him, and no countesses ever again would read sonnets, or hum them aloud before the mirror late late after a desultory party, and no woman would ever again try to make up her mind, and for all I know, no mirror ever again would stand clear on a wall, calm in its gilt oval (that shape in which a woman sees herself most truly), it is false or feeble to think of food. Yet there are times, especially at night, when the house seems to be alive with a midnight appetite, an astral

Dagwood planning strata of unlikely foods, a sweaty old rich Rossini turning from music to, what? What would Rossini have eaten late at night, when the sky was too bright with stars, too sculptural with cloud, too clever with nightingales, for him to go to bed, however pretty his companion or compliant nurse, what would he eat, while his kidneys ached and the moon sashayed across what he already knew must be one of the last lovely spring midnights of his life? . . . Would he tinkle a bell, and a cadre of diligent, unsurprised servants fall into *sorbet* formation, or pull a mousse providently be-forehand from the ferns around the ice-blocks in the double doored chest? After the truffles and gooseliver and cockscombs at dinner, what would pacify the, not hunger, truly, the *need*, a pure spiritual need it may be, yes, Rossini's utter desperate agonizing need to take into himself now before sleep or love or dying, just one more morsel of this after all adorable cosmos. He is silent as he watches them carry first a table, then a silver tray with Something on it across the dark lawn. We shall not stay to see him lift the cover.

But in this house some similar tendency, less ele-gant, less poignant, for our sun will never fall from the sky, true?, it's always here, yes?, always as it is now, supreme and ordinary, forever, ewig, ja? some similar nudge of appetite troubles the hours between midnight and sleep. What will it be? Not then the earnestness of cheese and oil and garlic and bread. A cookie, a biscuit, something heavy, crumbly as earth, dry, not juicy, not sweet, not very sweet . . . no chocolate, understood?, a dry fine halfsweet crumbly cookie, . . . no deceptive froth or teeth-aching icing, just the fine dry halfsweet, less than halfsweet cookie. That comes to mind some rare nights, when Bhutan becomes the half of an immense peanut butter cookie, say. But then a voice from the hallway cries: Man! Do not eat your world! Man! Man! Man!

—Robert Kelly, *A Line of Sight*

The Golden Toothpick of Omar Khayyam

Omar Khayyam, it is said, used to clean his teeth with a golden toothpick while poring over the metaphysical work of Avicenna, the *Shifa*. When he reached the chapter "On the One and the Many" he placed the toothpick between two pages and said: "Call the almoner, I wish to make my testament." And having made his will, stood up, prayed, and ate and drank no more—and died.

—Leo Kanner, in Tahir Shah's
The Middle East Bedside Book

◈ A Ravening Performance,
a Ravishing Love

◈ *In Milorad Pavić's* Dictionary *of the* Khazars, *Kalina and Petkutin fall in love, then share a theatrical meal with a dead but responsive audience:*

They ate by turns from the same fork, and she drank wine from his mouth. He caressed her until her soul groaned within her body, and she worshipped him. . . . But she thought to herself: "The moments of my life are dying like flies gulped down by fish. How can I make them nourishment for his hunger?"

◈ *I'll leave you in suspense, not terror, as to how the performance ends, but this is how it begins after the blood sausages have had their time on the cinders:*

" 'Don't summon the dead!' Kalina warned him. 'Don't summon them—they'll come!'

"As soon as the sun had departed from the theater she removed the mushrooms and blood sausages from the fire and they began to eat. The acoustics were perfection itself, and each bite they took carried singly and with equal clarity to every seat, from the first to the eighth row, but everywhere, in a different way, echoing the sound back to them at center stage. It was as if the spectators whose names had been carved into the fronts of the stone seats were eating together with the couple, or at least were greedily smacking their lips with every bite. One hundred and twenty pairs of dead ears were eavesdropping at pricked attention, and the entire theater was chewing along with the married couple, hungrily sniffing the aroma of the blood sausages. When they stopped eating, the dead stopped too, as if a morsel had got stuck in their throat, and they waited tensely to see what the young man and woman would do next. At such moments, Petkutin was especially careful not to cut his finger while slicing the food, because he had the feeling that the smell of human blood might throw the spectators off balance and that, as quick as a shooting pain, they might attack him and Kalina from the gallery and tear them apart, driven by their two-thousand-year-old thirst. He felt himself shudder, drew Kalina toward him, and kissed her. She kissed him, and they could hear the sound of 120 mouths kissing, as though those in the gallery were kissing too."

Do you think I've invited too much death into this book? Berlioz's bouncing head, Monsieur Le Prince at Versailles, the skeleton with crust of bread, the suicide hors d'oeuvres? The deadly light bulbs of the Queen of Siam? Balzac snuffed out by his coffeepot, Catalonian rats crunched to bits by a carnivorous tree? Eating is killing for life, and I will not sweeten the truth. Ravens and crows have traditionally been associated with the dead, and not only in Poe's "The Raven," so the crow who landed on our cover came from far away and for an endless stay. Trees have died to make this book: can't you feel their leaves quaking as the pages turn? Death, after all, is a ravenous muse indeed, the surest to have its plate of muscles and bones. But also its books, art, and music, which death takes from us as we live, that we will outlive ourselves.

Friday I tasted life.
It was a vast morsel.

—Emily Dickinson

Biographies of Authors Quoted and Anecdoted

Guillaume Apollinaire (1880–1918) Born Guillaume Albert Wladimir Alexandre Apollinaire de Kosdrowitzky in Rome, Apollinaire was a poet and mouthpiece of Cubism, writing on art and clarifying the significance of the changes afoot in Paris before and during the First World War. Among artists and writers, he was everyone's friend and kept everyone friendly; Gertrude Stein wrote that after his death (of a head wound, from the war), there was no one to keep them all together. His Cubist poems included snatches of overheard café conversation and sounds of the street, much as Braque's and Picasso's paintings would take in a scrap of newspaper. Apollinaire was incredibly active during these years, and in *Alcools* he celebrated Paris in poetry that caught the rhythm and light of the city in this brilliant time. *The Heresiarch and Co.*, from 1910, is the collection of stories from which we borrowed "The Romantic Cigar." *The Poet Assassinated,* also stories, came six years later.

Marcel Aymé (1902–1967) French author of novels, short story collections (*The Proverb and Other Stories, Across Paris and Other Stories*), and children's stories. His short stories often combine an otherworldly angle or element with an ironic, satirical look at such human weaknesses as hypocrisy. In "The State of Grace," an improbably pious, virtuous man wakes up with a halo, which he seeks to rid himself of by descending into the most sordid debaucheries. The ravenous muse insists I mention the title story of *Across Paris*, which concerns the clandestine and risky business of transporting two suitcases of contraband pork across Occupied Paris through one long night.

Isaac Babel (1894–1947) spent most of his life (taken from him, under Stalin) in Odessa, separated from his wife and daughter, who lived in Paris. Babel first discovered literature in a French class taught by a Breton. At the age of fifteen, in Odessa, he wrote his first fiction in French, with Maupassant as a model. Babel's stories bring the port of Odessa, with its Jewish community, other ethnic cultures, exotic foods, spices, and characters, pungently alive. To write his Moldavanka stories, he moved into this part of Odessa inhabited by two thousand bandits and thieves. Konstantin Paustovsky, on first reading one of Babel's early Moldavanka stories, wrote: "Its freshness hit you in the face like a splash from a siphon." He refused to write under the dictates of the state, so his output was all early—*Red Cavalry, Odessa Tales,* and *Benya Krik, The Gangster and Other Stories*—and all written with the greatest care. Konstantin Paustovsky describes how Babel would put a story through twelve painstakingly different drafts.

George Balanchine was born Georgi Melitonovitch Balanchivadze in St. Petersburg in 1904. He left Russia for Paris, where he joined Diaghilev's Ballets Russes in 1924, under the new name Diaghilev gave him. He came to New York in 1933 and with Lincoln Kirstein co-founded the School of American Ballet and the New York City Ballet, for which he choreographed many ballets; he remained its director until his death in 1983. Bringing an extraordinary musicality, modernity, precision, and astonishing versatility to dance, Balanchine has been called "the Mozart of choreographers"; and what's more, he loved to cook, as he did often for composer Igor Stravinsky, his longtime collaborator with whom he created some of his most original ballets. *Balanchine: A Biography* by Bernard Taper is an intensive, intelligent study, made right in the midst of Balanchine's creations, through rehearsals and choreography.

Honoré de Balzac (1799–1850), called the "Napoléon of letters" in France, wrote the sprawling (in time and volumes) *Comédie humaine* and the best-sellers that preceded it, *Eugénie Grandet* and *Père Goriot*. Balzac is an honorary member of the Slavic Gastronomes, since he traveled to the Ukraine to visit Eveline Hanska, whom he married just before his death, and spent most of the last two years of his life in Wierzchownia with her.

Roland Barthes (1915–1980)   Semiology wasn't his idea in the first place, but he was one of its leading proponents, setting the tone and seeing the signs in literary France and beyond from the 1960s on. His books include *Writing Degree Zero, Mythologies, A Lover's Discourse,* and *S/Z. The Rus-*

tle of Language contains "One Always Fails in Speaking of What One Loves." And I am finding it difficult to write of the writers I most love. I nearly said "of the lovers I most write." That too.

Charles Baudelaire (1821–1867) is very dear to the raven/crow on the cover, for Baudelaire was the first writer with a respectful audience to assess Poe's significance, and pronounce him significant, making Poe much more esteemed and appreciated in France than in the United States, perhaps even to this day. And the young Julio Cortázar, whose Cronopios are eating time in *this* book, translated Poe's stories into Spanish. But back to Baudelaire: he was a leading art and literature critic and poet of Symbolism and Decadence in France, no doubt having the most fun when indulging in both at once. His book *The Flowers of Evil* lent its name, in the singular, for an exhibition on tobacco at the Bois de Boulogne in 1994.

Andrei Bely (1880–1934), the pseudonym of Boris Nikolayevich Bugayev, was a central figure of the Russian Symbolist movement of the 1920s; his glory was at its height immediately before and after the revolution. He was influenced by theosophy, publishing his scientific-mystical manifesto of color correspondences, "Sacred Colors." Bely believed that a literary work becomes more profound as it moves toward music. *Petersburg* is his undisputed masterpiece. Also available in English are his novels *The Silver Dove* and *Kotik Letayev.* A glimpse of Bely in the émigré milieu of Berlin can be seen in Nina Berberova's memoirs, *The Italics Are Mine*. He returned to Moscow, crushed.

Mikhail Bulgakov (1891–1940) grew up in Kiev and was a medical doctor before devoting himself to writing; to supplement his income, he also worked with the Moscow Art Theatre. His satirical novel about the theatre, *Black Snow,* portrays Stanislavsky in his later years. Two other Bulgakov novels available in English are *Heart of a Dog* and *The White Guard. The Master and Margarita* was not published until twenty-five years after his death.

Anthony Burgess (1917–1993) A remarkable example of death's ravenous musing: informed in 1959 that he had one year to live, Burgess set out to finish a book or two before being borne away. He proceeded to write another fifty books, compose symphonies, and live in Monaco and Lugano with his Italian wife, Liana. His subjects and genres cut a wide swath, and I find the earthiness in his writing most palpable: while reading "Hun" in *The Devil's Mode,* my nostrils twitched along with Attila's bride's at the smell of roasted horseflesh that sustained him and clung to his skin. *One Hand Clapping* made me feel sick every time his characters ate, their diet was so revolting. But many eat with great pleasure and finesse on his thousands of pages. Burgess's novels, witty and erudite as well, include *Honey for the Bears, A Clockwork Orange* (where milk, *moloka,* is the juvenile delinquents' favorite drink), and *Earthly Powers. Homage to Qwert Yuiop,* a collection of essays on art and life (including a rare put-down of M. F. K. Fisher), and *A Mouthful of Air,* on language, are among his many nonfiction works.

James Burke was born in 1936 in Londonderry, Northern Ireland. Was I ever surprised to find that out; and yet now think, no wonder all that waggish charm and feel for language are there to carry his cross-discipline message through our televisions. Presented first in that form, the material is also wrapped up in his books *Connections* and *The Day the Universe Changed,* making accessible science and related subjects "closed by nature of their very vocabulary." And so through language, image, roaming around, dramatizing events in the history of thought, trade, discoveries, and scientific and cultural interconnections that are by no means evident, Burke illuminates the past and the present, letting us look at things with him in what to most of us is quite a new light.

Piero Camporesi, a professor of Italian literature at the University of Bologna, has a unique approach to history (Robert Darnton, of *The Great Cat Massacre,* is one colleague working in a similar vein) and a distinctive writing style. Camporesi looks at documents many scholars don't touch to revive the sense and sensations of life in earlier times and cultures, then puts them across in a style so intense that they also revive the reader. His replete and descriptive titles will give you a palpable idea of what his books explore: *The Fear of Hell: Images of Damnation and Salvation in Early Modern Europe*; *The Incorruptible Flesh: Body Mutation and Mortification in Religion and Folklore*; *The Magic Harvest: Food and Folklore in Society*; as well as the book on chocolate that I encountered in French, whose English title is *Exotic Brew: The Art of Living in the Age of Enlightenment.*

Elias Canetti was born in 1905 in Russe, Bulgaria, into a family of Ladino-speaking Sephardic Jews, a family he brings vividly alive in *The Tongue Set Free: Remembrance of a European Childhood*—including a reclining grandmother, smoking all day long à la Turque. In Ruse, a crossroads of cultures, the humblest inhabitants spoke four languages. *The Torch in My Ear* continues Canetti's autobiography in Vienna, with its coffeehouses, a recitation of "The Raven," and the legendary Karl Kraus. In 1981, while living in England, he was awarded the Nobel Prize for Literature.

Antonin Carême (1784–1833), an abandoned child (one of twenty-five: he was left by the city gate after a farewell meal with his father at a tavern), became a great chef and *patissier*, for the prince regent in England, Czar Alexander in St. Petersburg, the court at Vienna, and the Baron de Rothschild, whose table, during Carême's seven years with him, was considered the best in Europe. His writings are erudite, elaborate, and majestic like his *patisseries*.

Leonora Carrington (1917–), a real beauty, left an upper-class English background (which she must have had in mind while writing her wickedly matter-of-fact story "The Debutante" in *The Oval Lady*) to join the Surrealists in Paris, and one Surrealist in particular, Max Ernst. Carrington painted and wrote—short stories, the play *The Flannel Night-Shirt* (staged in lighted windows of a building on stage), and then *Down Below,* a moving account of her mental breakdown (brought on when Ernst, as a German citizen, was interred by French authorities in 1939) and her recovery in Spain. She moved to Mexico during the war, continuing as a painter and becoming a photographer too, and friends with Spanish painter Remedios Varo. I've been told that for a while, Carrington also mastered the art of living as an amphibian. The muse wants me to get out of the water, though, and into the dining room. The climax of "The Debutante," during the ball in her honor, is the dinner party that shocks the high-class guests: the debutante herself, you see, still in her own room upstairs, had kidnapped a hyena from the zoo (whom she'd befriended and tutored in French), fitted it out with the maid's face, and sent the creature down in her place, wearing her dress and high heels.

Lewis Carroll (1832–1898), whose other, everyday name was Charles Dodgson, wrote *Alice's Adventures in Wonderland*, *Through the Looking-Glass*, *Sylvie and Bruno*, and *The Hunting of the Snark*. A mathematician, he also composed games and puzzles of logic. Carroll visited Russia in 1867, his first and only trip abroad. Early in his émigré life, after studying at Cambridge, Vladimir Nabokov was commissioned by a Russian publisher in Berlin to translate *Alice in Wonderland*. His biographer Brian Boyd writes: "To make the book a self-sufficient plaything for Russian children he staged a gleeful raid on the toys and tags of a Russian nursery: the French mouse that came over with William the Conqueror became a mouse left when Napoleon retreated, Alice became Anya, trivial puns became quadrivial. The twenty-three-year-old Nabokov's *Anya v strane chudes* has been rated the best translation of the book into any language."

Blaise Cendrars (1887–1961) The first time I heard his name, it was somewhat weighted down with trunks, as it was off and on throughout his life. I say somewhat because he was floating, on one ship or another, for he was a constant traveler, accompanied by his poems, telling the story as he went along. During the Occupation, while living in Aix-en-Provence,

Cendrars raised culinary and medicinal herbs to sell and was also a beekeeper. As he told Michel Manoll: "I'm interested in bees because they make me a lot of money." When Cendrars met Sonia Delaunay in Paris, it was collaborative love at first sight: hearing some of his poem *Prose du Transsibérien*, she disappeared into another room and designed a foldout book for it. Other poetry by Cendrars will be found in *Panama, or the Adventures of My Seven Uncles*, and *Easter in New York*. Greatly admired by his pal Henry Miller, Cendrars' novels are free of literary pretension and allusion and are a far cry from Marcel Proust.

René Char (1907–   )   Can't you tell by his lines about olives that René Char is from the South of France? The Vaucluse, to be precise. The Midi suffuses his poetry, even through the Second World War, when Char was a brave leader in the Resistance. Albert Camus wrote, in his preface to the German edition of Char's *Poésies*, "Char, caught up as we all are in the most confusing history, has not been afraid to maintain and celebrate within this history the beauty for which it has given us so desperate a thirst."

Anton Chekhov (1860–1904) was one of Russia's best known and loved playwrights, and his plays have never left the stage: *Uncle Vanya, The Sea Gull, The Cherry Orchard, The Three Sisters.* Chekhov was also a master of the short story, and a very prolific one at that: numerous collections and translations never go out of print, while during his lifetime every literate Russian was reading them hot off the press. Chekhov wrote his first light pieces to help support his family, whom he continued to take care of all his life. Soon the entire country was his family. As a doctor, he treated thousands of patients gratis, and when he had the means, he undertook building projects all over Mother Russia: libraries, clinics, schools. His health, weakened by tuberculosis, eventually required that he live in a warmer climate—Yalta—so he was in Moscow only briefly for various productions of his plays. In Chekhov's story "Victory Celebration," 1883, the bliny seem to leap into characters' mouths quite of their own volition. Three years later Chekhov was lamenting that writing stories no longer felt like eating bliny, an effortless act, indeed! The muse was no longer feeding him lines.

Barbara Comyns (1909–1992) was an artist and the author of eight offbeat novels characterized, as Ursula Holden has written, by an "almost ferocious innocence." *Who Was Changed and Who Was Dead, The Skin Chairs, The Vet's Daughter,* and *Our Spoons Came from Woolworths* are four of her books published by Virago Press.

Julio Cortázar was born in Brussels in 1914, grew up in Argentina, and lived most of his adult life in Paris, where he died in 1984, after completing *les Cosmonautes sur l'autoroute,* a collaboration with his wife, Carol Dunlop. His books include *Cronopios and Famas, The End of the Game and Other Stories,* novels *The Winners, Hopscotch, 62: A Model Kit,* and what he called his collage novel *Around the Day in Eighty Worlds.* Cortázar brought major innovations to the novel genre, and his language goes right into your bloodstream (he did feel an affinity with vampires). Cortázar, like García Márquez and Lezama Lima, is translated into English by Gregory Rabassa, who was very proud of his pear tree on Long Island. Covetous of the one pear it was bearing at last,

Rabassa ensured his possession of it by smearing the tree trunk with Vaseline, against which the equally covetous squirrels had no flying chance.

Guy Davenport   Born in South Carolina in 1927, living in the South once again, Guy Davenport has a mind that goes everywhere: his erudition and curiosity seem boundless, and the reader bounds right along with him, so engagingly does he write and think—in two collections of essays, *The Geography of the Imagination* and *Every Force Evolves a Form*. In an essay about Henri Rousseau, "What Are Those Monkeys Doing?" he illuminates the drama and the primate pranksters' bemused faces in Rousseau's painting *Merry Jesters* by taking a good look at the soda siphon bottle in the foreground, mistakenly identified as a milk bottle since 1906. Elsewhere Davenport recounts how he extinguished a fire in Jean-Paul Sartre's pocket with a glass of water at a Paris café (*"Monsieur, vous brûlez,"* Sir, you are on fire). Paul West wrote in *Sheer Fiction*, volume two of *The Geography of the Imagination*: "Davenport, as a child, took his Sunday portion of roast beef, macaroni pie, and peach cobbler, but now gets by on fried baloney, Campbell's soup, and Snickers bars—whereas what he festively dines on are books, chaps, and even maps. These 40 courses are a sample of the Belshazzar's feast that goes on in his head." Davenport also writes poetry and fiction. *Tatlin!* and *Eclogues* were followed by more short stories in *Apples and Pears*.

Emily Dickinson   (1830–1886)   "I'm nobody. Who are you?" In her own words, here she is—should we say any more? Unpublished in her lifetime spent in Amherst, Massachusetts, she left her "letter to the world": 1,775 poems.

Fyodor Dostoevsky (1821–1881) went from being a radical who served time to the other end of the political spectrum. I recall, in *The Idiot*, merciless conversations at the dinner table, dominated by Aglaia's garrulous and meddlesome mother. "The Crocodile" is a wacky departure for him and welcome divertissement for us. Major works include *Notes from Underground*, *Crime and Punishment*, *The Brothers Karamazov*, and *The Possessed*, which was dramatized by Russian director Yury Lyubimov in London and Paris (nothing like his Taganka Theater production of *The Master and Margarita*, complete with special effects and Margarita's night flight for "Satan's Rout," according to my Ukrainian friend Boris, who saw it twelve times, enthralled).

Sergei Dovlatov (1941–1990) grew up in a mixed Armenian-Jewish family in Bashkiria, Soviet Union, lived in Leningrad before and after a brief fling with the freer intellectual climate of Estonia, and emigrated to the United States in 1978, where he settled in New York City. While living in Leningrad, he worked briefly as a guide in the Pushkin Museum. His writing is both satirical and autobiographical, not necessarily both at once. Besides *The Compromise*, you can read *The Invisible Book* and *The Suitcase*, a collection of eight stories, which was going to press as Dovlatov was dying. A favorite pair of sentences in *The Compromise:* "All the same, I want to know what you experienced in the North. To put it figuratively, what was the tundra silent about?"

Alexandre Dumas, *père* (1802–1870) was a prolific writer of drama, novels, travel, and *le Dictionnaire de cuisine*. With his early dramas he helped bring in the French Romantic movement. His output was impressive (and quite a contrast to his son's, as our anecdote chez George Sand reveals): he could write for fourteen hours straight with hardly a correction to make. *The Three Musketeers* and *The Count of Monte-Cristo* are a couple of his best known novels; many have been turned into film more than once. Robert Louis Stevenson said of Dumas's storytelling style: "light as a whipped trifle, strong as silk."

Lawrence Durrell (1912–1990) wrote the *Alexandria Quartet* with astonishing speed, and, at a more leisurely pace, Mediterranean travel books. There's also his sensuous *The Black Book* and my favorite, *Pope Joan*, about the pope who was discovered to be a woman while going into labor on the Vatican steps. With the most delightful scholarly footnotes. Durrell, Henry Miller, and Anaïs Nin called themselves the Three Musketeers of La Coupole, the café on boulevard Montparnasse where they used to meet.

Luigi Colombo Fillia, creator of the Simultaneous Dinner, was a member of the Italian Futurists: the rowdiest proponents of Futurism in Europe, the quickest to glorify war (as hygiene), castigate pasta (and all bourgeois conventions of the table), idolize machines (hence such items as ball bearings in their recipes), and assert (our muse agrees here) that human experience is liberated by art in everyday life. They issued manifestos (the first in 1909) and scenarios, staged publicity tours, and in 1912 went to Paris expecting to be greeted like the Three Wise Men with their crisp suits and hats, wild socks and ties, and swagging locomotion. Very loco it all was, and much more romantic than the Cubists, from whom they learned a thing or two. In 1932, still going at full ebullition, Filippo Tommaso Marinetti, the movement's leader, published *La cucina futurista,* many of whose recipes are pure poetry, feeding all the senses and setting the scene (a cockpit, a blue-green gilded forest, a table that's a sheet of crystal on shining aluminum legs, illuminated with constantly varying light from beneath) as well as choreographing all the colors and gestures involved. *The Futurist Cookbook* proposes such "dinner programmes" as Dinner of White Desire, Geographical Dinner, Extremist Banquet (with French windows electrically opening onto a series of smells). Recipes include Elasticake, Devil in Black Key, Fisticuff Stuff, Captive Perfumes (drop of perfume inside balloons), Libyan Aeroplane, Network in the Sky.

Gustave Flaubert (1821–1880) "Madame Bovary, *c'est moi*" (Madame Bovary, that's me). We can imagine this as an exchange with Emily Dickinson (see above), although it was really George Sand with whom Flaubert corresponded, and who addressed him as her "old troubadour." Flaubert was writing *Un Coeur simple* for her when she died, in response to her advice: "Write something more down to earth that everyone can enjoy." Flaubert also wrote *Sentimental Education* and *Salammbô*. Recommended reading: Julian Barnes's *Flaubert's Parrot.*

Stephen Fry is the author of two novels, *The Liar* and *The Hippopotamus,* and *Paperweight,* a collection of his witty, insightful, satirical, and serious "articles and itemries" (some wonderful pieces on language and also a new Sherlock Holmes story) originally published in London's *Listener* and *Daily Telegraph.* He is also half the comic genius writer-actor duo *A Bit of Fry and Laurie,* from BBC-Television, and if you've missed all that, I weep for you. You may know him as Jeeves in BBC's *Jeeves and Wooster,* Wodehouse dramatized, but I prefer him where he writes his own lines and metamorphoses, which he enacts so splendidly.

Eduardo Galeano was born in Montevideo, Uruguay, in 1940, and now lives there again after years of exile (Argentina, Spain) and wandering far from aimlessly throughout Latin America: he has devoted his heart and mind to political freedom, his voice to speaking for those oppressed, and not only in this century. His *Memory of Fire* trilogy chronicles, in short, packed pieces, the history of Latin America—through anecdote, legend, fact, and fatality, a work at once dark and illuminated. *The Book of Embraces*, drawing on his travels and sojourns, traces these themes *and* celebrates friendship in all its forms and faces, and is sometimes comical, sometimes ironic, sometimes tragic, touching at every turn. His latest book is *Walking Words*, in a similar spirit.

Gabriel García Márquez (1928–   ), born in Colombia, made way in literature for even more imagination (not that anything would stop it), beginning with the block of ice and Aureliano's golden fishes in his novel *One Hundred Years of Solitude*, for which he won the 1982 Nobel Prize. Then came *Autumn of the Patriarch* and *Love in the Time of Cholera*. Collections of his shorter fiction include *No One Writes to the Colonel and Other Stories*.

Stella Gibbons (1902–1989), first a journalist, then a novelist, was born in London and wrote poetry, short stories, and novels. *Cold Comfort Farm* was her first novel, which she impishly marked with asterisks beside the headiest passages. In this laugh-aloud and instantly popular work of fiction, the level-headed Londoner Flora Poste sorts out the destinies of her caricature rural cousins, the Starkadders.

Nikolai Gogol (1809–1852), with *Dead Souls* and his short stories, took Russian literature to a place it had never been before him, and it's never been the same since. His story "The Overcoat" (inspired by an anecdote that he heard at a tea party in St. Petersburg) influenced Dostoevsky's early novels, and is also flapping its sleeves behind Mandelstam's story of Parnok in *The Egyptian Stamp*. Gogol's short stories come in all sorts of collections and translations, and the more I am seeing of the Russian language, the more I find myself reluctantly concurring with the owner of The Village Voice Bookstore in Paris, who put me soundly in my place with: "How can you say you like Russian literature when you don't even know Russian?" You'll just have to take the translators' words for it, though, unless learning Russian is in your own next few five-year plans. If you want to further follow Gogol in a fantastic direction, a bit of fictional biography, Tommaso Landolfi's story "Gogol's Wife" will make your eyes pop out.

Witold Gombrowicz (1904–1969) was the rapscallion scion of Polish upper-middle-class almost-aristocrats. Following publication of his novel *Ferdydurke*, an outrageously defiant book, Gombrowicz lived as Witoldo for twenty-five years in Argentina. In his diary, a report for our muse: "This is how the supper at the Bioy Casareses' ended: nowhere. Like all suppers consumed by me with Argentine literature." On his return to Europe, he achieved international recognition, and lived in southern France until his death, when he went on living multilingually. An exchange of letters between Gombrowicz and Bruno Schulz, his contemporary in Poland, was published in the spring 1987 *Antaeus*.

Edmond (1822–1896) **and Jules** (1830–1870) **de Goncourt** were brothers far apart in age, looks, and temperament who nevertheless remained remarkably close throughout their lives. The journal they kept together, in which their prose is difficult to distinguish, is full of gossip, the record of an age, a fine place for eavesdropping. They collaborated on the journal, novels, and art history until Jules's death.

Václav Havel (1936–   ) was a playwright, prisoner, chronic critic of the Czech Communist regime through the seventies and eighties, and then—*voilà!*—the Velvet Revolution, and suddenly he became the Magic Lantern Theatre president of Czechoslovakia. Havel wrote his *Letters to Olga* during his imprisonment: the only writing he was permitted, and that severely censored, so he had to find circuitous ways to say certain things. Still, I don't think the comments about Earl Grey tea have any hidden meanings, such as that little old ladies in England were tunneling their way to his prison cell for the abduction they'd arranged with him.

François Hébert (1946–   ), I am sorry to say, has not been translated into English. He's a Québecois writer whom I first met in Paris as the author of prose poems, *Barbarie*, and of *Histoire de l'impossible pays nommé Kzergptatl, de son roi Kztatzk premier et dernier et de l'ennemi de celui-ci le sinistre Hiccope 13 Empereur du Hiccopiland*. Later from this fantastic mind (Hébert's) came *Monsieur Itzago Plouffe*. Hébert is also editor of the literary review *Liberté* and professor of literature at the University of Montréal, and the next-to-the-last husband of Julio Cortázar's last wife, Carol Dunlop. *le Dernier Chant de l'avant-dernier dodo* is a collection of modern, timeless fables, the point of the title being that it's the last song of the *next-to-last* dodo that matters, as the last song of the last dodo would have considerably less meaning, with no one to understand it.

James Joyce (1882–1941) was born in Dublin, which he portrayed through fifteen stories in *Dubliners,* the final one, "The Dead," written in Trieste. In *Portrait of the Artist as a Young Man* Joyce introduced Stephen Dedalus, who would meet his spiritual father, Leopold Bloom, in *Ulysses,* written in Trieste, Zürich, and Paris. Thanks to Sylvia Beach and an unusual arrangement, *Ulysses* was published in Paris in 1922—one of the great events of publishing history. Then again, I could simply say that James Joyce lay down where all the ladders start in the foul rag and bone shop of the heart. And then he wrote *Ulysses* yes and each episode in a different style yes and yes, yes he did write more after that. When I read a book, I often feel impelled to eat what its characters are eating, and, not having tasted kidneys since landing at Bremen in 1959, and having read half of *Ulysses* before my Paris homecoming of 1982, I had Leopold Bloom with the cat and the kidney much in mind while visiting a Uruguayan sculptor and putting in my request for dinner, since lots of meat and guests were arriving. And what was the name of that Uruguayan who indulged my literary-culinary desire? Why, Leopoldo, of course. Joyce felt that readers should spend their lives with his books, so I don't want to foreshorten the fun awaiting you. If your life is long enough, you can go on to *Finnegans Wake,* the only book Yolanta had with her when she went into the hospital far from Baden-

Baden's *konditorei*, and instead of reading it she slept and dreamed.

Ismail Kadare, born in the southern Albanian city of Gji-vokastïr in 1936, drew generously from childhood memories during the Second World War (occupation in rapid succession by Italians, Greeks, then Germans) in writing his novel *Chronicle in Stone*. Kadare found fame first as a poet, then as a novelist, as he continues to be, and his books, published and well received throughout Europe, have been best-sellers in France. *Chronicle in Stone*, told with such immediacy, and through a child's eyes, is a rare chance to experience a community in Albania, with its local characters and their personal drama running alongside the larger commotion of war. Kadare's other novels include *Broken April, The Palace of Dreams*, and *The Concert*. Exiled from Albania, he now lives in France.

Franz Kafka (1883–1924) was born in Prague to German-Jewish parents, died of tuberculosis in a Viennese sanatorium, and was buried in the Jewish cemetery of Prag-Straznice. By day a wretched civil servant who certainly couldn't fit in, by night Kafka was the author of short stories, including "The Metamorphosis" and "A Hunger Artist," and three novels that were all unpublished during his life: *Amerika, The Trial*, and *The Castle*. Bruno Schulz, one of our muse's favorites, translated Kafka into Polish. The ravenous muse is flapping its wings again, saying I must mention Kafka's story "Research of a Dog": a dog thinking about food and where it comes from wonders about the relationship between food and his constant need to pee.

Robert Kelly (1935–   ) has been prolifically published for several decades by Black Sparrow Press—volumes of some of the finest American poetry being written: *The Mill of Particulars, Finding the Measure, The Loom, A Line of Sight,* and *The Convections.* No, not confections, although some of these poems are good enough to eat. Collections of fiction came along, too, including *Cat Scratch Fever* and *Queen of Terrors.* Kelly teaches at Bard College in upstate New York.

Omar Khayyam, a brilliant mathematician and astronomer who lived in twelfth-century Persia, was at odds with the religious and social restrictions of his time, and *The Rubaiyat,* poems, were his way of having it otherwise and praising a different sort of life, one that delighted the senses. Jorge Luis Borges wrote a delightfully speculative story about Omar Khayyam's translator, Edward Fitzgerald, and the third person the two men became across cultures and centuries.

José Lezama Lima was born in 1910 in Cuba, where he's not been in great favor since the publication of *Paradiso,* as it treats the taboo subject of homosexuality openly and doesn't so much as mention the revolution. I learned while finishing my book on punctuation that Lezama Lima was asked by his editor why his book was punctuated in such odd places. He explained that he had asthma, and he inserted commas, other pauses, when *he* was gasping for breath: a different rhythm altogether established by his lungs. Julio Cortázar, who helped get *Paradiso* published and noticed once it was, wrote in *Around the Day in Eighty Worlds* of Lezama's unusual work: "my own reading of *Paradiso,* as of all of Lezama, begins by expecting the unexpected, by not demanding a novel, and then I can concentrate on its content without useless tension, without that petulant protest that arises from opening a cabinet to get out the jam and discovering instead three fantastic vests."

René Magritte (1898–1967) was a Belgian Surrealist whose room certainly had a view of its own: just try looking through his windows. Throughout his life as an artist, Magritte, usually wearing a suit, painted in a corner of his dining room, cleaning his brushes before dinner. But it's not true that Madame Magritte ever grilled that mermaid-in-reverse of his and served it on a Sunday evening.

Osip Mandelstam (1891–1938), one of Russia's greatest voices, was a poet at the time of Anna Akhmatova and fellow Acmeists and with them enjoyed the early exhilaration of the revolution, until writers found themselves doomed by their own words: their souls. Most of Mandelstam's poems would be lost today, except that his wife, Nadezhda, memorized every single one, saving them and her husband's memory from oblivion. He was imprisoned several times for minor indiscretions, and died in a prison camp. Clarence Brown's introduction to *The Noise of Time*, Mandelstam's prose works, is very informative both biographically and aesthetically, and Nadezhda's two immense books, *Hope against Hope* and *Hope Abandoned*, much more widely read than her husband's poetry, tell the full story as she knew it. While in prison and also at an asylum, Mandelstam was convinced that he was being poisoned, and refused to eat what little food he was given, stealing bread from fellow prisoners or inmates so as not to starve to death. It's chagrining to recall this while reading his sublime "Conversation about Dante" in his collected prose and his poem with poison in bread.

Vladimir Mayakovsky, a Georgian boy, was born in 1893 and committed suicide in 1930. After his death, his brain was removed and borne away in a cloth-covered bowl, "like a cheese pudding," Yury Olesha says. In his autobiographical "I Myself," Mayakovsky announces, "I'm a poet. That's why I'm interesting." Well, he was also a playwright, a graphic artist, a satirist of the conventional art forms of his day, and a leading figure in the Cubist movement in Russia in 1911–12. The ravenous muse noticed that his *A Cloud in Pants* shows the poet Igor Severyanin in the shape of a long-stemmed wineglass (we know from Olesha that the wine Mayakovsky would have drunk from it/him was Abrau-Dyurso). Mayakovsky wrote the first Soviet drama, *Mystery-Bouffe* (*bouffe* being French slang for food: grub), which includes some fantastic scenes with that *bouffe*: in Heaven a cloud is milked, another sliced, and when the *very* assorted travelers, the play's characters, see locomotives and cars (wreathed in rainbows) bearing bread and salt, they are afraid the bread will bite them.

W. S. Merwin (1927–   )   His books of poetry include *The Carrier of Ladders, The Rain in the Trees, The Drunk in the Furnace,* and *The Dancing Bears. Houses and Travellers* stands apart from his other collections, as he has new rhythms and space in the form of the prose poem, sometimes verging on story, often as mysterious as "The Taste" on water. Merwin has also translated poetry from Spanish, French, and other languages.

Silvia Monrós Stojaković, an Argentine who has lived in Beograd for many years, writes stories with the same leaps and astonishing fusions as her letters, and has also written books on Julio Cortázar, Salvador Dali, and Gala. Having made Serbo-Croatian her own wild animal of a language, out-distancing, outnuancing, outdeepening most Serbs, she has also translated Cortázar's *Hopscotch* and Jorge Luis Borges's literature lessons into Serbo-Croatian. What's more, Silvia has shared in the same lineage of champion borzois that you've seen posing with Milorad Pavić on the dust jacket of *Dictionary of the Khazars.*

Michel Eyquem de Montaigne (1533–1592) It was Montaigne who gave the essay its name in French and English—a form in which he excelled. Our muse is on speaking terms with him because his travel journal is rich in observations of both everyday life and more cerebral subjects *and* because Montaigne, who lived near Bordeaux, wrote surrounded by vineyards. What would he have thought of Basil Fawlty's "It's always a pleasure to meet someone who appreciates the boudoir of a grape?" Montaigne wants to say something about this biographical section of our book: "We are all made up of fragments, so shapelessly and strangely assembled that every moment, every piece plays its own game. There is as much difference between us and ourselves as between us and others."

Vladimir Nabokov (1899–1977) That line of Montaigne's recalls the book in which V. Sirin, writing in Russian while living as an emigré in Berlin and Paris, became a writer in English: *The Real Life of Sebastian Knight*, which Nabokov wrote in the bathroom at night while his wife and child slept in the only room of their Paris apartment. Once they were in the United States, Nabokov's wife, Vera, saved *Lolita* from the incinerator, where he was headed with it when the book was still a child of several chapters. Had I started quoting Nabokov's novels in *The Ravenous Muse*, I wouldn't have known how to stop, nor would I have wanted to know, which is why I stuck to his lectures on Russian literature and his mother's mushrooms from *Speak, Memory*. Several other favorites: *Pale Fire, Pnin, Ada, Look at the Harlequins.*

Flann O'Brien (1911–1966) This was the pen name of Brian O'Nolan, one of Ireland's comic geniuses. He set his genius to work in *The Poor Mouth*, written originally in Gaelic and under the Gaelic nom de plume Myles na Gopaleen, to portray the hard lot of Ireland's impoverished (potatoes are the only food available throughout this both satirical and tragic Bildungsroman). His wildly plotted, colorfully spoken novels, ranging from lyrical to farcical, include *At Swim-Two-Birds* (the most complex of his works), *The Dalkey Archive*, and *The Third Policeman*. While at the University College in Dublin, he published an obscene epic in Old Irish, for which he went unpunished because the prosecuting authorities and the president of the college could not read the salty tongue of their forefathers. Graham Greene wrote of *At Swim-Two-Birds* in 1939: "I read it with continual excitement, amusement and the kind of glee one experiences when people smash china on the stage."

Yury Olesha (1899–1960) spent much of his childhood and later years in Odessa and also lived in Moscow. My friend

Boris inscribed the book of his we found together: "Olesha is the writer who scares me the most. He was a great person, but he did *not* do anything. Maybe that's why I got out from Russia." For like Isaac Babel, Olesha answered the Five-Year Plans and Stalinism with silence. This came after a smashing success with his novel *Envy*, until the Party realized that *Envy*'s readers were identifying with the wrong characters (one of whom is a repulsive wizard in the food industry). Olesha also produced a collection of short stories and a play before shutting up his subjectivity and eloquent metaphors. *No Day without a Line*, written during the last six years of his life, is what happened when Olesha, despairing of this silence, vowed to write one line a day—which amounted to several paragraphs a day of memories, vignettes, reflections on literature and his literary contemporaries. His earliest memory: eating slices of watermelon under a table, and he's wearing a girl's dress. Russian scholar, essayist, and novelist Victor Shklovsky wrote of *No Day without a Line*: "Olesha tested each word on his teeth to see if it were gold, looked at it through a magnifying glass, turned it this way and that before he set it in a sentence."

Konstantin Paustovsky (1892–1968), born in Moscow, grew up in Kiev, where his boyhood imagination was set ablaze by the tales of his grandfather, a descendant of the Zaporozhian Cossacks. After two years at the University of Kiev, in 1913 Paustovsky went to Moscow, but that was just the beginning of his wanderings and mixed métiers, whereby he acquired much experience, as a tram conductor (not in *The Master and Margarita!*), ambulance driver, factory worker, fisherman. In the late 1920s he returned to Moscow, switching to writing as a journalist, essayist, novelist, and author of short stories. His fiction moved from the romanticism and exoticism of the first collections to reflections of everyday life, which romanticism nevertheless pervades. It was his richly evocative autobiographical works that brought him international readership in the 1960s—*The Story of a Life* and *Years of Hope*, which are at once personal and historical: a record of turbulent times touching all lives. Ordinary people from his many encounters are here, as are Paustovsky's literary contemporaries: Babel, Bulgakov, and others.

Milorad Pavić (1929–   ), born in Beograd, is a professor of literary history at the University of Beograd and a leading Serbian poet. His extraordinary novels bring us not only a new way of writing, but also of reading, as he means them to; and yet when I read the first pages of his lexicon novel to be translated into English, it felt like an ancient form of literature also, and not only because of its subject. I wrote my friend Silvia, "This is how literature is *supposed* to be." Even the word *original* was finding its meaning again. *Dictionary of the Khazars* opens with an explanation gently prefaced by a promise that the lexicographer "will sit down to write these notes before supper, and the reader will take them to read after supper. Thereby, hunger will force the author to be brief, and gratification will allow the reader to peruse the introduction at leisure."

S. J. (Sidney Joseph) Perelman (1904–1979) developed a genre all his own, pieces of wit and abashing vocabulary, punning titles ("The Hand That Cradles the Rock," "A Farewell to Omsk"—a favorite with our Slavic Gastronomes), dazzling displays of rhetorical devices and adventurous sentence structures. An outstanding embodiment of his hilarious virtuosity is "No Starch in the Dhoti, S'Il Vous Plaît," the correspondence between a pandit in India and the Paris *blanchisserie*, Pleurniche et Cie., where he sends his laundry.

Joan Perucho (1920–), a Catalan author born in Barcelona, has written poetry, short stories, novels, art criticism, and gastronomic explorations. The suppression of the Catalan language (Catalonia was autonomous during the Spanish Republic) under Franco forced Perucho to keep his literary activities secret for many years, but as things lightened up, and then Franco died, Perucho emerged resplendent with his gifts and literary output.

Fernando Pessoa (1888–1935) is considered Portugal's greatest twentieth-century poet, although his work was largely unpublished until after his death. But how many deaths are we talking about? In 1914, he began to produce works by writers of his own creation, complete with biographical and astrological backgrounds, philosophies, and literary styles. These personalities he (?) called heteronyms, twenty of which led quite loquacious and productive lives, and one of whom, Fernando Pessoa, was no more valid or dominant than the rest. Among these flourished Alberto Caeiro, of simple joys, the pastoral fellow; and Alvaro de Campos, a precocious existentialist with the energy of Marinetti, an engineer on a tanker who speaks the language of machines.

Frederic Prokosch (1908–1989), an American-born novelist, spent much of his life in Europe. Albert Camus wrote that Prokosch "has invented what might be called the geographical novel." This geography includes *The Asiatics*, *The Skies of Europe* (set in Paris, Munich, Austria, and Barcelona before the Second World War), and *The Missolonghi Manuscript* (three fictional notebooks of Lord Byron, as if written in the Greek village, Missolonghi, where Byron died). Prokosch was gifted with a memory in his ears that made the marvel of *Voices: A Memoir* possible—a collection of chance encounters and conversations throughout his life with W. H. Auden, James Joyce, Giorgio de Chirico, Wallace Stevens, a Balkan spy. In Rome, he runs into Dylan Thomas and the two impulsively drive to the ancient seaport of Ostia, where Thomas strips and plunges into "that dirty old sea," imagines himself a charioteer, a little girl, a witch with a cauldron into which he would stir various parts (modesty forbids me to say which parts of whom) of Stephen Spender, Edith and Osbert Sitwell, and several stellar critics of poetry. One chapter in *Voices* is "The Death of Chekhov," getting there before that train and those oysters, receiving the news at Badenweiler with a princess who was there at the time.

Marcel Proust (1871–1922), perfectly nocturnal and universally acknowledged the greatest French writer of the twentieth century, chronicled la Belle Epoque in his cork-lined room, living on coffee and croissants except for an occasional dinner or *sortie*. His masterpiece *A la Recherche du temps perdu* unwinds from the first memory infusing a madeleine taken with his *tisane*. In an extensive essay, *On Reading*, with his style already apparent (long unbroken paragraphs that go on for pages, melodious language flowing with ideas and images), Proust complains about how the act of reading is interrupted by meals, and others' preoccupation with them: "Before lunch, which, alas! would put an end to reading, one had two long hours still. . . . often, before lunch, those who were tired and had shortened their walk . . . began to arrive in the dining room. They would all say, 'I don't want to disturb you,' but began at once to come near the fire, to look at the time, to declare that lunch would not be unwelcome. . . . Some, without waiting any longer, would sit ahead of time at the table, at their places. That was real desolation, for it would be a bad incentive to the others as they arrived to make believe that it was already noon, and for my parents to pronounce too soon the fatal words: 'Come, shut your book, we're going to have lunch.' "

Raymond Queneau (1903–1976) was a founding member of the College of 'Pataphysics and OuLiPo, Ouvroir de littérature potentielle, the workshop for potential literature. His books in English include *The Bark Tree, Pierrot Mon Ami, The Sunday of Life, Exercises in Style,* and *Zazie in the Métro,* and all mix street talk with cerebral sophistication. *Exercises in Style* takes the same two-part banal anecdote (told in its edible variation here) on a Paris bus and puts it through many transformations: olfactory, painted with colors, self-conscious and confused, tactile, lofty, argot, epic poetic, libretto, to name a handful of these voices. Queneau's innovations with genre, structure, language, philosophy have refreshingly influenced contemporary French literature and from there jumped boundaries of every kind, on land or in the mind.

Pascal Quignard (1948–), born in Verneuil, France, lives in Paris, where he works as an editor at Editions Gallimard. *The Salon in Württemberg* is the first of his novels to be published in English; let us hope the rest are coming—*Carus, les*

Tablettes de buis, and *les Escaliers de Chambord*. It doesn't surprise me, after reading this one novel, that he has also written nonfiction on music and literature.

Rainer Maria Rilke (1875–1926), born in Prague, lived and studied in Bavaria; Munich was an artistic center nearly the equal of Berlin in these years. In 1902 Rilke went for the first time to Paris, initially as Rodin's secretary (and it was he who found the house on rue de Varenne where Rodin came to live and is still housed—his museum, that is). *The Notebook of Malte Laurids Brigge* is Rilke's novel based on his earliest experiences in Paris. It's for *Sonnets to Orpheus*, *The Duino Elegies*, and other poetry that Rilke is supremely known. He died of leukemia in Valmont.

Jacques Roubaud (1932–) is a professor of mathematics (quizzes for the reader in *The Princess Hoppy* hint at his mathematical and logical wizardry) at the University of Paris X Nanterre. Not *Non*terre. He is very much on this earth, writing poetry, translating American poets and Lewis Carroll's *The Hunting of the Snark*, and writing the Hortense novels, which are published in English by Dalkey Archive Press: *Our Beautiful Heroine*, *Hortense Is Abducted*, and *Hortense in Exile*. Editors and publishers (of books) and authors' agents should all read the chapter "I Am Not Madame Bovary" in *Hortense Is Abducted*. Yet another novel, *The Great Fire of London*, offers *Roubaud's Law of Butter Croissants*, which seems quite sound to me, both morphologically and texturally. Roubaud is a virtuoso member of OuLiPo, the workshop for experimental literature founded by Raymond Queneau and François Le Lionnais, where Georges Perec played too.

Raymond Roussel (1877–1933) was born in Paris at a very good address, and although he traveled extensively (rarely leaving his stateroom or hotel room), he created the worlds in his novels almost entirely out of his own imagination. It was not only his methods of keeping his handsome head of hair from graying that were unusual: Roussel derived a unique and rigorous system for the development of each of his novels, which he explained in his small and fascinating work *How I Wrote Certain of My Books.* Those books include *Locus Solus* and *Impressions of Africa.* Jean Cocteau called Roussel "the Proust of dreams," and "genius in the pure state" with potent spellbinding capacities.

Salman Rushdie (1947–)   Rushdie's first big splash was *Midnight's Children,* which begins with the birth of independent India and the novel's narrator. *Shame* followed, and then *The Satanic Verses.* Since the startling start of his long strange holiday from predictably visible existence, Rushdie has produced three more marvels: for his son and the children in all of us, *Haroun and the Sea of Stories*; a collection of essays, *Imaginary Homelands*; and the nine stories that take us *East, West.*

Donatien Alphonse François, marquis de Sade (1740–1814) gave his name to *sadism,* although in fact his libertines are much more detached than sadists tend to be. Like Omar Khayyam in twelfth-century Persia, Sade was at odds with the hypocrisy of his time, so he took it on by writing (mostly in prison) variations on the novel *Justine,* with its vision of evil, which I read by accident at the age of sixteen, having mentioned to a friend (I was reading Durrell at the time), "I've lost my *Justine*." "Oh, I'll loan you mine," he said, and so my corruption commenced.

Louis de Rouvroy, duc de Saint-Simon (1675–1755) you will meet, along with many others, in *The Age of Magnificence: Memoirs of the Court of Louis XIV by the Duc de Saint-Simon*. This is a selection from Saint-Simon's generous, intimate, astute, and amusing accounts of life among the nobles at Versailles, where he had "an insultingly tiny room." After Saint-Simon died, it took some time, once these writings were discovered—forty-three volumes—for their literary merit to be recognized, but now they are an acknowledged treasure of the written world.

George Sand (1804–1876), born Amantine Aurore Lucile Dupin, wrote many books, fiction and memoirs, as well as drama, at a very quick pace, but I get the impression that her true art form was friendship, sustained through letters when not in person. And what friends! Delacroix, Franz Liszt, Alfred de Musset, Chopin, whose mistress she was for years. Her correspondence with Flaubert is full of frank discourse: even the bear bares his soul, and what's more, he addresses *her* as "Dear Master." In Paris you can visit George Sand at the Musée de la Vie Romantique, which you'll walk through some of the sleaziest streets of the city to reach. You turn a corner, walk a few paces, and suddenly you are gazing down a leafy pathway into serenity and light. The museum was the house of painter Ary Scheffer, who captured Pauline Viardot's affection, much to Turgenev's chagrin, but now it's inhabited by George Sand's spirit, and her material possessions, too.

Erik Satie (1866–1925), from Calvados, came to Paris well before the famous banquet honoring the painter Henri Rousseau, where he and fellow Norman Marie Laurencin sang Norman songs and someone ate someone else's straw hat. Satie was an original in more than his musical compositions, which include the one for piano called *Three Pieces in the Form of a Pear*. Satie worked on many different scales: he even wrote a miniature opera for marionettes. Our muse insists I mention one of twenty snatches that make up *Sports et divertissements: Chorale inappétissant* (Unappetizing chorale). For the Ballets Russes he wrote the music of *Parade*, with libretto by Jean Cocteau, choreography by Leonide Massine, sets and costumes by Pablo Picasso. To mark events of importance, however slight, Erik Satie wrote himself letters, which he sealed, mailed, and opened on delivery, and the best way I know of to get to know him is by reading *Satie through His Letters*, with drawings, photos, selections lovingly assembled by Ornella Volta, who has the keys to Satie's *placard* (closet) in Paris, and his musical scores. In "At Table," Satie writes that the table, round or square, is fit for worship, and that of all his memories as a guest, his lunches with Debussy were the most charming and unforgettable.

Bruno Schulz (1892–1942) was a Polish writer, Jewish, gunned down at the age of fifty by an SS officer in an Aryan section of Drohobycz. He left an unfinished novel, *The Messiah*, which disappeared, and two collections of stories that are so interrelated they could be considered novels: *Sanatorium under the Sign of the Hourglass* and *The Street of Crocodiles*. Both evoke his childhood in a home pervaded by his father's madness (and also inhabited by tailors' dummies)—a father who in one episode/dimension metamorphoses into a crab and is served for supper. The stories are set in the vanished world of the Jewish community in the small town of Drohobycz, where Schulz spent most of his life. Schulz's prose is a delirious pleasure to read, almost hallucinogenic in its imagery and sensations. One other book is available in English: *Letters and Drawings of Bruno Schulz*.

George Bernard Shaw (1856–1950) was born in Dublin and moved to London in 1876. He set about his own course of autodidacticism before becoming a music critic for the *Star*, thence drama critic with other publications, in all of which his writing could be savage, as he said exactly what he thought. His plays, forthright and controversial in subject matter—prostitution (*Mrs. Warren's Profession*), adulterous feelings in a young vicar's wife (*Candida*), housing conditions, other social and political issues—always come with lengthy, witty prefaces setting the scene and polemics. *Arms and the Man* is a farce set in a Balkan country.

Charles Simic, born in Beograd in 1938, bred and fed on American poetry while growing up in Chicago and New York—as recounted in his *Wonderful Words, Silent Truth*—is a prolific and Pulitzer Prize–winning poet. Simic's books of poetry include *Return to a Place Lit by a Glass of Milk*, *White*, *The World Doesn't End*, *Hotel Insomnia*, and *Dimestore Alchemy: The Art of Joseph Cornell*. He has also translated volumes of Slovenian and Serbian poets.

Edith Sitwell (1887–1964) proclaimed her avocational interests to be music, silence, and reading: isn't that a fine sandwich? When *Facade* was first performed in London, it was greeted with such incomprehension that Sitwell said, "I had to hide behind the curtain. An old lady was waiting to beat me with an umbrella." Among Sitwell's works are *The Canticle of the Rose: Selected Poems 1920–1947*; and *Facade: An Entertainment with Poems*. T. S. Eliot rated Sitwell one of the most important voices of twentieth-century English poetry. She was exquisitely attuned to sound and music in the language: her poems are to be read aloud.

Gertrude Stein (1874–1946), who was right there when modern art was first asserting itself, with Picasso's *les Demoiselles d'Avignon*, Cubism coming and going, and what came after it, was also an avatar of modern letters, influencing more writers than are aware of it. Her writing was doing something new and strange from the beginning: *Three Lives*; her portraits; *Tender Buttons*, the idea for which came to her as she sat in the Alhambra of Spain watching the swallows swooping in and out. She would render the rhythms of the visible world. Stein, born in Oakland, California, spent nearly all her life in France—Paris when there wasn't a war driving people to the countryside. I also recommend reading the first sentence of her novel *The Making of Americans*.

Sara Suleri (1953–) teaches English at Yale University. *Meatless Days*, her first book, re-creates the world of her childhood in Pakistan, and does so in a language unashamed of itself, daring to be dense and complex, summoning feelings of the past and the present to revisit family relationships, make sense of the colonial experience and of being far from that world now. Throughout *Meatless Days*, food is ever-present, speaking for Suleri's concerns as it is prepared and consumed, playing an almost allegorical role in this literary memoir.

Tatyana Tolstaya was born in Leningrad, now Petersburg, in 1951, and lives in Moscow as well as the United States, where she has taught literature and creative writing at several universities. Following an eye operation, Tolstaya couldn't read for three months; when the privilege returned and she considered how to enjoy it, she realized that what she longed to read was her *own* stories, which she then began to write. Her two short story collections published in English are *On the Golden Porch* and *Sleepwalker in a Fog*. From a postcard Silvia (of "El Masoquista, Brave Old Planet") surprised me with, after I sent *her* both books: "Now it's me that's being on a South Pacific island, accidentally nothing less than Bali, but the book I took from home is the Tolstaya one containing the story of that nurse that dreams about the supreme god in the shape of a surgeon while wearing a graceful robe from GDR [German Democratic Republic] under the pink light from the Yugoslav lamp, though I also enjoyed like crazy the other stories, specially 'Loves Me, Loves Me Not' which I've read while sitting under a palm tree on the beach."

Leo Tolstoy (1828–1910), Tolstaya's great-uncle, went from count to muzhik (he took to dressing like a peasant) on his estate at Yasnaya Polyana. Tolstoy was the author of "The Death of Ivan Ilyich," *The Kreuzer Sonata*, *War and Peace*, and *Anna Karenina*. In the latter, the author introduces Anna's brother Steve while he dreams of a dinner party on tables of glass, the tables are singing *Il mio tesoro*, with little decanters on top that are at the same time women. Nabokov describes Tolstoy as "a robust man with a restless soul, who all his life was torn between his sensual temperament and his supersensitive conscience." My Serbo-Croatian book tells me how to say "Tolstoy's flight from Yasnaya Polyana was fateful for Russian literature," and here's the story: at the age of eighty, Tolstoy left home to seek a simple life closer to his ideals, heading for a monastery, but died along the way in the waiting room of a remote railway station.

Henri de Toulouse-Lautrec (1864–1901) was an artist with short legs and big eyes who of all painters and lithographers is most intimately associated with the dance halls of Montmartre, the Moulin Rouge, the Moulin de la Galette, and all the girls who danced there, such as la Goulue and Jane Avril. He did posters of them that were plastered all over Paris, and he loved to dress up in costumes.

Michel Tournier, born in Paris in 1924, spent his childhood in Saint-Germain-en-Laye, where the early chapters of Pascal Quignard's *The Salon in Württemberg* are set. Tournier has worked in publishing, radio, and television, and his interest in photography informs his novel *la Goutte d'or* (The golden droplet). His books in English include two novels, *The Ogre* and *The Four Wise Men,* and *The Fetishist and Other Stories.*

Ivan Turgenev (1818–1882)   The author of *Sketches from a Hunter's Album,* capturing the character (of serfs) and landscape of rural Russia (their anti-serfdom meaning not apparent till they were published together), Turgenev spent most of his life away from Russia, in Baden-Baden and Paris, then building a dacha at Bougival on the Seine to be near the singer Pauline Viardot. Turgenev's major works were the novels *Rudin, A Nest of Gentlefolk,* and *Fathers and Sons*—seen by many Russians as too Westernized. In France, Turgenev felt less misunderstood, was sometimes lionized (appropriate to the impressive mane that handsome head bore straight into his death), and enjoyed the friendship of such eminent writers as those he dines with in this book.

Rebecca West (1892–1983) wrote journalism, biography, criticism, fiction, satire, travel, and history, and blazed her own trail through interweaving these genres and concerns. In 1937, sensing that Yugoslavia's cultural complexity held a vital key to Europe's destiny, West was compelled to take a long and thoughtful journey through those layers and landscapes. The result was *Black Lamb and Grey Falcon*. More than a tour of a Balkan country, this book is a tour de force. Sensations and observations en route, conversations with friends/guides Constantine and Valetta (one Serb, the other Croat) and many people along the way (Moslems, Macedonians, Sarajevo Jews, Gypsies, a belly dancer with whom West takes a lesson), reflections at night as she's reliving the day, history, literature, and legend come across vividly, brilliantly—never flagging over 1,150 pages.

Ludwig Wittgenstein (1889–1951), a Cambridge don from a cultivated, wealthy Viennese family, considered his immense inheritance a hindrance and gave it all away. He was one of the most influential philosophers of the twentieth century, but he was so acutely aware of words and meaning, language and thought, that I'm afraid to say anything more. Having read about his birthday cake riposte, you can see why I tremble, pondering how to present his person.

Permissions Acknowledgments

Index